IMAGES
of America

RALEIGH
NORTH CAROLINA'S CAPITAL
CITY ON POSTCARDS

Cards extending greetings were popular with both collectors and those buying cards to send. Some of these cards were customized for individual cities. "Greetings from Raleigh" is written across the bottom with paint and sprinkled with material that glitters. The person addressing the card added "NC, Nov. 22, 1906," and it was sent to Miss Ethel Dickerson, RFD #3, Oxford, North Carolina.

IMAGES
of America

RALEIGH

NORTH CAROLINA'S CAPITAL
CITY ON POSTCARDS

Norman D. Anderson and B.T. Fowler

ARCADIA

First printed in 1996
Reprinted in 2000

Published by Arcadia Publishing,
an imprint of Tempus Publishing, Inc.
2A Cumberland Street
Charleston, SC 29401

Printed in Great Britain.

For all general information contact Arcadia Publishing at:
Telephone 843-853-2070
Fax 843-853-0044
E-Mail arcadia@charleston.net

For customer service and orders:
Toll-Free 1-888-313-2665

Visit us on the internet at http://www.arcadiapublishing.com

Copyrighted 1907, by Tichnor Bros., Inc.
Pat. applied for.

This "Seeing Raleigh, N.C." card is a double card. When opened, an accordion folder reveals twenty-two postage-stamp-size views of the Capitol, the Governor's Mansion, local colleges, and other Raleigh attractions. The circular paper clip on the far right side of the card was used to keep it from coming unfolded when mailed.

Contents

Raleigh, North Carolina

Original Boundaries

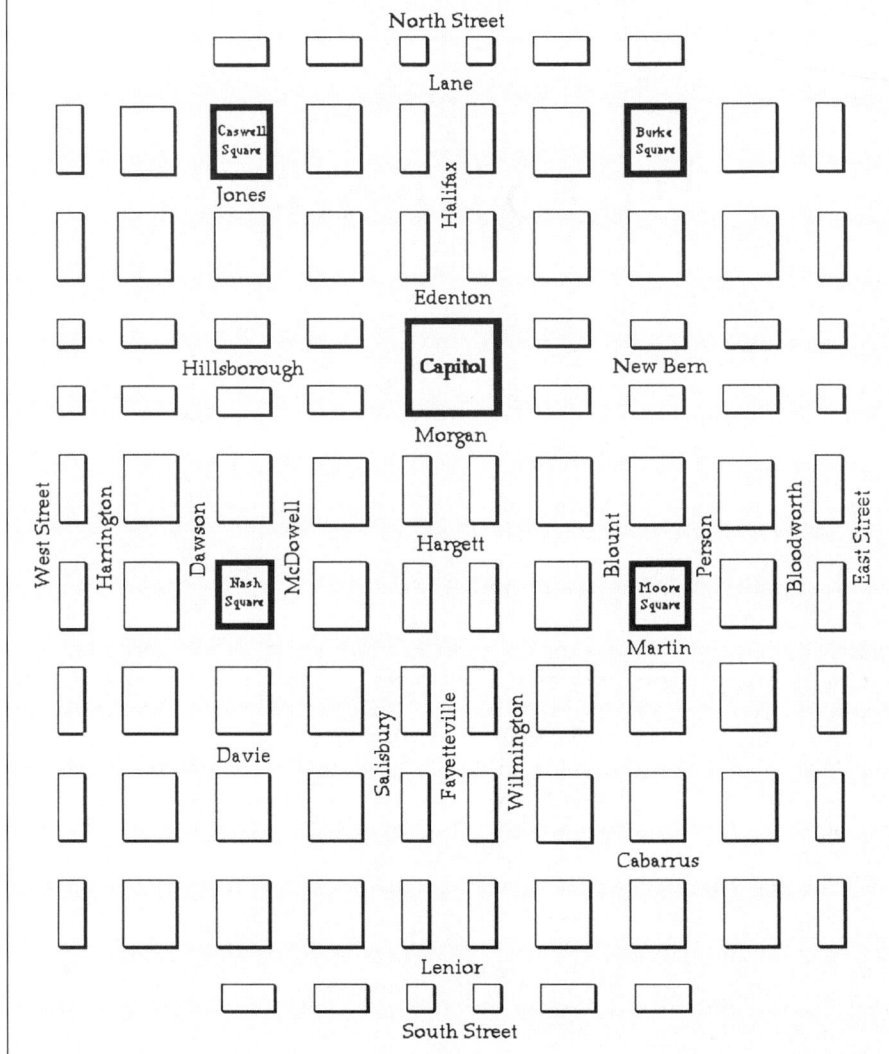

North Street

Lane

Caswell Square   Burke Square

Jones

Halifax

Edenton

Hillsborough   **Capitol**   New Bern

Morgan

West Street   Harrington   Dawson   McDowell   Hargett   Blount   Person   Bloodworth   East Street

Nash Square   Moore Square

Martin

Davie   Salisbury   Fayetteville   Wilmington

Cabarrus

Lenior

South Street

Eight of the streets near the Capitol were named after the state's court districts in the 1790s: New Bern, Edenton, Morgan, Salisbury, Halifax, Wilmington, Fayetteville, and Hillsborough. Other streets were named after the nine members of the commission who selected Raleigh as the capital: Bloodworth, Blount, Dawson, Hargett, Harrington, Jones, Martin, McDowell, and Person. Still others were named after Senate Speaker William Lenoir, House Speaker Stephen Cabarrus, and General William R. Davie. Lane Street was named after Colonel Joel Lane, from whom the land was purchased for North Carolina's new state capital.

A 6-acre site was designated as the site for the Capitol and four blocks, equal distance from Capitol Square, were set aside as parks. Two of these parks, Moore Square in the southeast and Nash Square in the southwest, are still in existence. The Governor's Mansion is located on Burke Square, northeast of the Capitol. Caswell Square, to the northwest, is occupied by state office buildings.

Introduction

The first picture postcards in the United States appeared in 1893 as part of Chicago's World Columbian Exposition. Postcards were quick to catch on and the first part of the twentieth century was the Golden Age of Postcards. The cards became instant collectibles, with millions of Americans filling albums and exchanging views with fellow collectors. And not only did postcards visually capture the diversity of our nation, but they provided an easy way to communicate with relatives and loved ones.

This selection of postcards, most of them published before 1930, illustrates many facets of life in North Carolina's capital city and in neighboring Wake County. A few cards, published in the 1930s and later, round out the story. The story, of course, is incomplete because of our being limited to the images preserved on postcards. For example, try as we might, no really good cards were found of the old airport on Fayetteville Road or the attractions at the state fair when it was across from the North Carolina State University campus. Also, we should add that, because of space limitations, some of the cards in this book have been reduced or cropped.

Examining postcard views is fun and the messages on the back add to their interest—providing news of an engagement, a new baby, or of the sender's safe arrival in Wilmington. Less pleasant communications tell of Uncle George's arthritis kicking up or hint at a romance gone sour. In a few cases, we have included some of these messages in the captions accompanying each card. In like manner, we have indicated the date a card was postmarked if this information seemed significant. We hope the postcards in this book capture the humor and light moments of the times as well as being informative.

We made our selection from a pool of over six hundred early postcards of Raleigh and Wake County. Although we have our own collections of local cards, it would not have been possible to assemble the remarkable compilation contained in this book without the generous assistance of fellow collectors and local institutions. In the case of borrowed postcards, an acknowledgment follows the captions for these cards. We wish to extend a special word of thanks to Durwood Barbour, who lent us more than three dozen cards from his wonderful collection of North Carolina cards, and to Maxine Fowler and Peggy Holliday for their encouragement and assistance while we were doing this book.

We hope you enjoy this postcard tour of early Raleigh and Wake County. If you are not already a postcard enthusiast, we invite you to join us in one of America's most popular pastimes.

About Postcards

As deltiologists, or postcard collectors, we are frequently asked about postcards. How long have picture postcards been produced? If a card is not postmarked, is there any way of estimating its age? Where can I find old postcards? What is the easiest way to determine the value of a card? And the list of questions goes on.

The term *postcard* describes privately printed cards that usually have a picture or message on one side, while cards printed by the government are called *postal cards*. Postcards have been around for about a hundred years and most can be classified according to their date of publication. The list to follow describes the types of cards that were produced during each era.

Pioneer Cards (1893–1898). These cards are quite rare; many of them are labeled as "Souvenir Postcards." Thus far we have not identified any pioneer cards of Raleigh and Wake County.

Private Mailing Cards (1898–1901). These cards have the term "Private Mailing Card" printed on the address side, usually along with the statement, "Authorized by Act of Congress of May 19, 1898." Private mailing cards of Raleigh and its neighbors in the county are very scarce and only a couple are included in this book.

Undivided Backs (1901–1907). Cards printed during this period are called *undivideds* because postal regulations did not allow a message on the address side. This was also true in the case of pioneer and private mailing cards.

Divided Backs (1907–WWI). On March 1, 1907, the U.S. Postal Service approved the divided back, which allowed for a message on the left side and the address on the right. Many of the undivided and divided back cards were published in England and Germany.

White Borders (WWI–1930s). After World War I, most of the cards sold in the United States were printed in this country. Since many of them had a white border, this term is used to describe cards published during this period. Some of the cards in this book fall into this category, but a few of them from this period lack the border.

Linens (1930s–1940s). These cards have a rough finish and were made using paper with a high rag content. A few of the most recent cards in the book, such as those of the bus station and Rex Hospital, are linens.

Chromes (1940s–present). These cards are printed mainly in color and most look like a photograph made from a colored slide. The two most common sizes are the standard 3 1/2-by-5 1/2 inches and the continentals, which are about 4-by-6 inches.

As with any classification system, there are exceptions. For example, real photo cards are printed on photographic paper with the word *Postcard* and a stamp box printed on the back. These are currently one of the most collectible categories and several of these cards of Raleigh and its neighbors in Wake County have been included in this book.

Flea markets, yard sales, antique shows, and friends with attics are all sources of postcards. Or you may want to attend one of the dozens of postcard shows held around the country each year. How much will you have to pay for postcards? The answer depends on the kind of cards you wish to collect, their age, and their popularity with other collectors. The price of the cards in this book would range from less than $1 to $20 or more. Among the least expensive are linen cards. The real photo cards of the Raleigh Fire Station, the highway commission truck, and of the small towns in Wake County carry the highest price tag. Of course you may luck out and find one of these prized collectibles in the 25¢ box!

One

Early History

After the Revolutionary War broke out, North Carolina was without a permanent capital. Finally, after much debate, a special commission selected a site in Wake County, which is near the center of the state. One thousand acres of land were purchased, of which 400 acres became the original city of Raleigh in 1792.

As shown on this card published to celebrate the city's sesquicentennial in 1942, North Carolina had another Capitol before construction began in 1833 on the present building. The first Capitol, a brick structure, was completed in 1796 and completely renovated in 1821–24. It was destroyed by fire on January 21, 1831. A night view of the east front of the present Capitol is shown in the lower right corner of this card.

(Above) This panoramic view of the State Capitol and Grounds was published as a black-and-white double card and was folded to be mailed. A message reads, "Am kept pretty busy with my team. I was all over the capitol and these grounds to-day." The card was postmarked on May 9, 1910, in Raleigh. A second postmark indicates it arrived the next day in Shippensburg, Pennsylvania. How is that for express mail and with postage of only 1¢?

North Carolina's capital city was named in honor of Sir Walter Raleigh. It was Raleigh who was responsible for establishing early English colonies in the New World in the late 1500s. Among those early settlements was a colony on Roanoke Island in the northeastern part of the state. What happened to these early settlers is not known; each summer an outdoor drama in Manteo tells the story of the "Lost Colony."

SIR WALTER RALEIGH

Born at Hayes Barton Devon 1552

Died at Whitehall London. 1618

GREETINGS FROM RALEIGH, N.C.

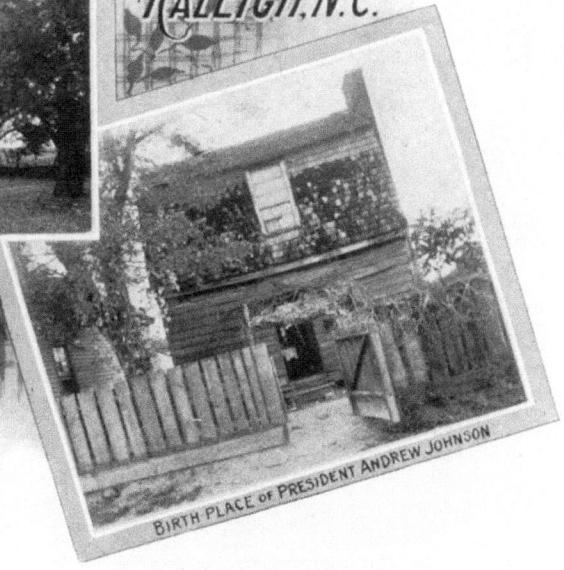

THE JOEL LANE MANSION, 1760

BIRTH PLACE OF PRESIDENT ANDREW JOHNSON

Not a very Stately mansion for a President to be born in. Still exists in the Park Geo.

The Joel Lane Mansion, once owned by the family from which land was purchased to establish Raleigh, was moved from its original location to 728 West Hargett, where it still stands.

The Johnson house was moved from near Capitol Square to Pullen Park in 1904. In 1975 the house was moved again, this time to the Mordecai Historic Park on Wake Forest Road.

This aerial view looking toward the east shows how the area around the Capitol looked in the 1930s. The First Baptist Church is visible in the lower left corner and Christ Church is in the upper center, across Wilmington Street from the Capitol. Fayetteville Street and the city's business district begins on the right side of the card.

The four views of Raleigh on this butterfly greeting card are the Vance Monument, the Governor's Mansion, the State Capitol, and the School for the Blind (when it was located on Caswell Square to the northwest of the Capitol). This card is in the PCK Series and is one of many butterfly cards published showing scenes from our nation's larger cities.

Two

The Capitol and State Government

Raleigh, N. C. State Capitol - Front View, showing Vance Statue.

The Capitol building shown here has served the state since 1840. The structure was built in the Greek Revival style of architecture, and the cost of construction and furnishings was $533,000. The stone for the building came from a local quarry about 1.5 miles east of the Capitol. It was brought to the site on an experimental railroad utilizing mule-drawn wagons. With a height of 98 feet, the Capitol was the tallest building in Raleigh at the time it was built. The governor's office is in this building; the general assembly, which met here for many years, moved to its new home on Jones Street in 1963.

"BIGGER, BUSIER, BETTER, RALEIGH"

"STATE CAPITOL, RALEIGH N.C."

The Capitol, state flag, and a cameo of Sir Walter Raleigh are used to promote a "bigger, busier and better Raleigh" on this card copyrighted in 1909. Sent to a Miss Smith in Philadelphia, the message in part reads, "This shows one side of the Capitol. The statue is the Late Senator Zebulon B. Vance. I hope sometime you will come down and let me show you through this magnificent building and the beautiful grounds of which we are very proud."

Night views of the Capitol were popular with postcard publishers. The message printed on the back of this white border card provides information about the outdoor lighting system that made these views possible: "There are nine circuits supplying the flood lighting system. The four facades are illuminated with special facade banks. The dome is floodlighted with eight 1,000 watt special flood light projectors."

Fourteen statues, memorials, and monuments have been placed on the Capitol grounds over the years and the older ones appeared on numerous early postcards.

The statue of George Washington was the first monument to be placed on Capitol Square. This bronze copy of Houdon's Washington was cast by Hubard from the marble original, which is in the Capitol in Richmond, Virginia. The George Washington Monument is located just outside the south entrance to the North Carolina Capitol.

The monument honoring Zebulon Baird Vance originally faced New Bern Avenue as shown on this card. Later it was moved to the southeastern section of the Capitol Square to allow the Three Presidents Monument to be placed on the east side of the Capitol.

Vance served as governor of North Carolina for three terms, as a colonel in the Confederate Army, and as a senator from 1879 until his death in 1894.

Vance Monument Raleigh N. C.

15

Worth Bagley Statue.

Ensign Worth Bagley, born in Raleigh in 1874, was the first American officer to lose his life in the Spanish-American War. The statue, to the west of the Capitol, was unveiled on May 20, 1907.

The handwritten message on the back of the card, postmarked 1909, attests to the sender's knowledge of history: "Tribute to the first hero to fall in the Spanish-American War. A Raleigh Boy. Graduate of Annapolis."

Raleigh, N. C. Glimpse of Capitol Square.

In this view of Capitol Square looking toward the northwest, the Bagley statue is on the right. On the left is the Confederate Monument and the First Baptist Church is in the background.

A Spanish naval deck gun is to the right of the Bagley statue. The gun was captured during the Spanish-American War and mounted here in 1908, a year after the statue was dedicated.

16

Motorists traveling east on Hillsborough Street toward the Capitol still get a view like this of the Confederate Monument. The three bronze statues on the monument represent the Confederate Infantry, Cavalry, and Artillery. Two 32-pound cannons are mounted on the sides of the monument.

Honoring the bravery of North Carolina soldiers who served in the Civil War, the inscription on the monument reads: "First at Bethel—Last at Appomattox."

MONUMENT TO THE NORTH CAROLINA WOMEN OF THE CONFEDERACY, PRESENTED TO STATE BY HON. ASHLEY HORNE. RALEIGH. N C.

The Women of the Confederacy Monument is located near the southwestern corner of Capitol Square facing Morgan Street. The monument was donated by Colonel Ashly Horne, who wanted to be sure the women of the Confederacy were remembered. The monument was dedicated on June 10, 1914. (Durwood Barbour.)

The United Daughters of the Confederacy sponsored this statue of Henry Lawson Wyatt. He was the first confederate soldier to die in the Civil War when he was killed on June 10, 1861, at Bethel, near Hampton, Virginia. The statue is located on the northwest corner of Capitol Square.

GROUP of MONUMENTS
IN THE CAPITOL GROUNDS,
RALEIGH, N. C.

This white border card features four of the statues on Capitol Square—Vance, Washington, Bagley, and McIver. The statue of Charles D. McIver, on the right, was dedicated in 1911 in recognition of the honoree's many contributions to education during the late nineteenth and early twentieth centuries. He was the founder of the State Normal and Industrial School, now the University of North Carolina at Greensboro. The McIver statue is located near the southeast corner of the Capitol.

18

The Governor's Mansion is located on Burke Square, two blocks east and two blocks north of Capitol Square. The mansion was constructed of bricks made by prisoners and the interior features native pine and other North Carolina products. This view shows the mansion about twenty years after it was completed in 1891. The brick fence surrounding the mansion today was added for security reasons in the late 1960s.

The Supreme Court and Agricultural Buildings originally were located across from Capitol Square on the northeast corner of Edenton and Salisbury Streets. The Supreme Court Building was designed by Colonel W.J. Hicks, who also was superintendent of the state penitentiary. Dedicated in March of 1888, the building housed the Supreme Court until it moved across the Capitol Square to its new home in the State Administration Building.

"The Old Red Brick Building," as it was known, was renovated in 1914. The two stories were converted into four by inserting new floors between the high ceilings of the two previous ones. The building presently houses the Department of Labor and now is known as the Labor Building. (Durwood Barbour.)

A 12207 Dept. of Agriculture, State Library and Museum, Raleigh, N.C.

we expect you Saturday - remember.

The Agriculture Building, in the foreground, housed the Eagle Hotel, the National Hotel, and Guion's Hall before it was purchased by the state in the 1880s. The State Library along with the State Supreme Court occupied the building on the left at the time this card was published. The Museum, now called the North Carolina State Museum of Natural Science, is on the right. This Agriculture Building was razed in the 1920s to make room for the new Agriculture Building that presently stands on the site. (Durwood Barbour.)

North Carolina State Museum, Agricultural Room

70-164

The North Carolina Department of Agriculture has maintained a museum since the 1880s. This postcard shows the kind of exhibits that were found in the Agricultural Room shortly after the turn of the century. This a very collectible postcard since it is an interior view, not many of which were published.

The first State Administration Building, built of Indiana limestone, was completed in 1913 at a cost of $325,000. Located on Morgan Street between Fayetteville and Salisbury Streets, the building's first tenants were the State Library, the Supreme Court, the North Carolina Historical Commission, and the offices of the Attorney General. The building was renovated in the late 1960s. Now known as the Ruffin Building, it houses the North Carolina Court of Appeals.

The Revenue Building at the northwest corner of Salisbury and Morgan Streets was occupied in 1926. Judging by the automobiles, this view was made shortly after the building opened. The old Raleigh Fire Station is shown on the left and to the rear of the Revenue Building.

The State School for the Blind was located on Caswell Square. The first part of the building was completed in 1848 as "a school for deaf and mutes." Blind students were admitted three years later. In 1895 the deaf students were moved to Morganton, and in 1898 the building was renovated and additions made. The School for the Blind remained at this location until the Governor Morehead School opened on Ashe Avenue in 1923. A portion of the building that housed the School for the Blind School at the corner of Jones and Dawson Streets is now called the Old Health Building and is still used as state offices.

The North Carolina Institution for the Deaf, Dumb and Blind established a department for black children in 1869. The students were housed for the first few years in space rented in the Washington School. In 1874, permanent buildings were erected on a one-acre site bounded by Bloodworth, South, Person, and Lenior Streets. The Raleigh Institute of Cosmetology was the last occupant of the remaining portion of the main building, which was taken down in 1992.

The North Carolina General Assembly in 1869 authorized "a penitentiary with a stockade and buildings to contain 500 cells." The first prisoners were housed in log cabins on the new prison grounds while an Ohio architect, Levi T. Schofield, designed the permanent building. The first block of sixty-four cells opened in 1875. The original complex, a four-story Gothic Revival brick building, was completed in 1884. The postcard view shows how the prison appeared from West Morgan Street a few years after the turn of the century.

Postcards showing interior views of prisons are quite rare. We probably will never know what led to these real photo postcards of the North Carolina's State Penitentiary—perhaps officials wanted to show off their modern facilities? The hand-printed caption on the card is a reminder that most public facilities were segregated at the time this photograph was taken in about 1910. (Manuscript Collection, Duke University.)

23

North Carolina's State Penitentiary had its own powerhouse as indicated by the caption. Note the striped prison garb on the man standing by the dynamo in the center of the picture. (Manuscript Collection, Duke University.)

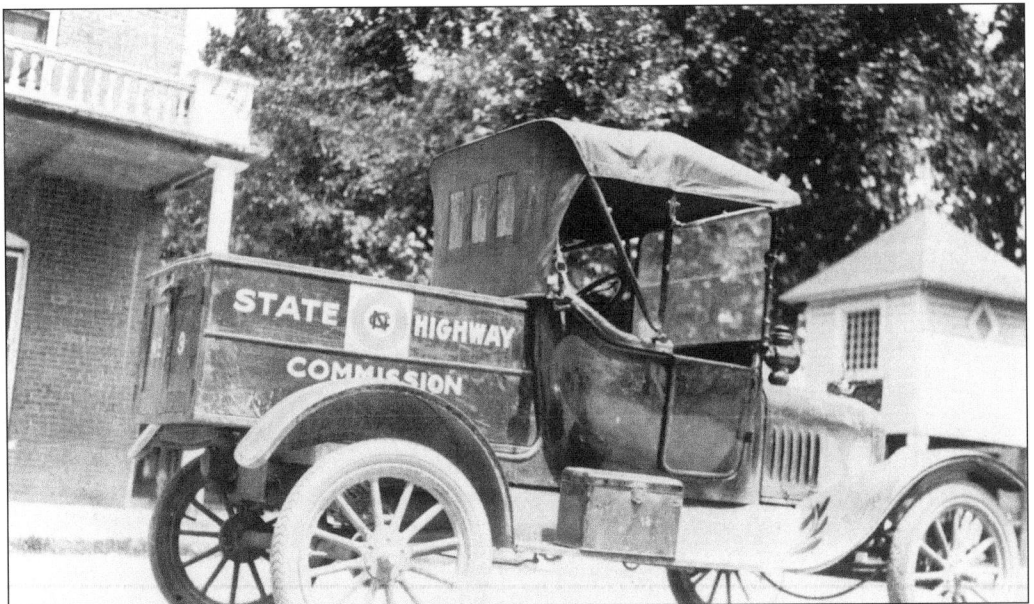

It seems fitting that the State Highway Commission would have some of the earliest state-owned motor vehicles. According to the sign on the back, this was truck No. 9. (North Carolina State Museum of History.)

Three
Old Downtown Scenes

Fayetteville Street, looking North, Raleigh, N. C.

The business district, state and local government buildings, and other downtown attractions are located on Fayetteville Street and a block or two on either side. Back when many of the early Raleigh postcards in this book were published, Fayetteville, Wilmington, Salisbury, and other downtown streets were crowded with buggies, wagons, streetcars, and later with automobiles. Today, Fayetteville Street is a pedestrian mall extending southward from the Capitol to the Civic Center, but a few of the old landmarks remain.

This panoramic view of Fayetteville Street was taken from its intersection with Davie Street looking north toward the Capitol. On the left is King's Business College, the Courthouse, and the Post Office. The Yarborough House is on the right side of this double card.

The buggy is in front of the Yarborough House, with the old Post Office across the street. Letters can still be mailed at the restored Century Post Office at the corner of Fayetteville and Martin Streets. The message of this card, postmarked October 10, 1913, reads, "1 of 12 from George E. Glover." This was during the period when thousands of collectors exchanged postcards and probably means the sender was sending another eleven of the Capitol City.

This card was postmarked September 4, 1918. By this time the traffic on Fayetteville Street was a mixture of buggies and automobiles. The sender wrote, "Mama and Dad came to Raleigh with me and we had a wonderful time. We stayed at the Yarborough and went all over Raleigh." The Yarborough is the second building on the right, just beyond the Municipal Building.

FAYETTEVILLE STREET, LOOKING SOUTH FROM STATE CAPITOL BUILDING, RALEIGH, N. C.   110870

By the time this white border card was published by James E. Thiem of the Office Outfitters, the Raleigh skyline was beginning to change. In addition to the several multi-storied buildings, Fayetteville Street had twin tracks for the streetcars and diagonal parking for automobiles.

Back when cotton was "King," Wilmington Street was a busy place in the fall months. The products of a farm family's summer toils were brought by wagon for sale to one of Raleigh's Cotton Merchants. As the sign shows, Coca Cola was 5¢. The large Coke sign makes this a very collectible postcard.

Cotton Merchants, Raleigh, N. C.

A familiar sight on South Wilmington in the early 1900s was the mule-drawn wagon loaded with cotton, waiting to be unloaded. The Commercial and Farmers Bank and the King Drugstore were two of the businesses located in that part of town. (Durwood Barbour.)

Alfred Williams and Company, in the 100-block of Fayetteville Street, was another early downtown business. Established in 1867, their building contained over 12,000 square feet of space and they used all three floors for their business. According to the printed message on the back of the card, they carried a "complete line of books, stationary, engraving, office supplies and furniture, typewriters, gold stamping, party and gift goods and more." The Alfred Williams Company also published postcards of early twentieth-century views of Raleigh. The company is now located at 1813 Capital Boulevard and goes by the name of Alfred Williams Office Supplies. (Willard Jones.)

ALFRED WILLIAMS & CO., 119 FAYETTEVILLE STREET, RALEIGH, N. C.

California Restaurant, Raleigh, North Carolina

The California Restaurant also was located in the 100-block of Fayetteville Street. A printed message on the back proclaims, "Famous for Old Fashion Southern Cooking, Established in 1900." The name came from the practice of selling fresh California fruit, but old-timers remember it as a great place to take a date for an ice cream sundae or shake.

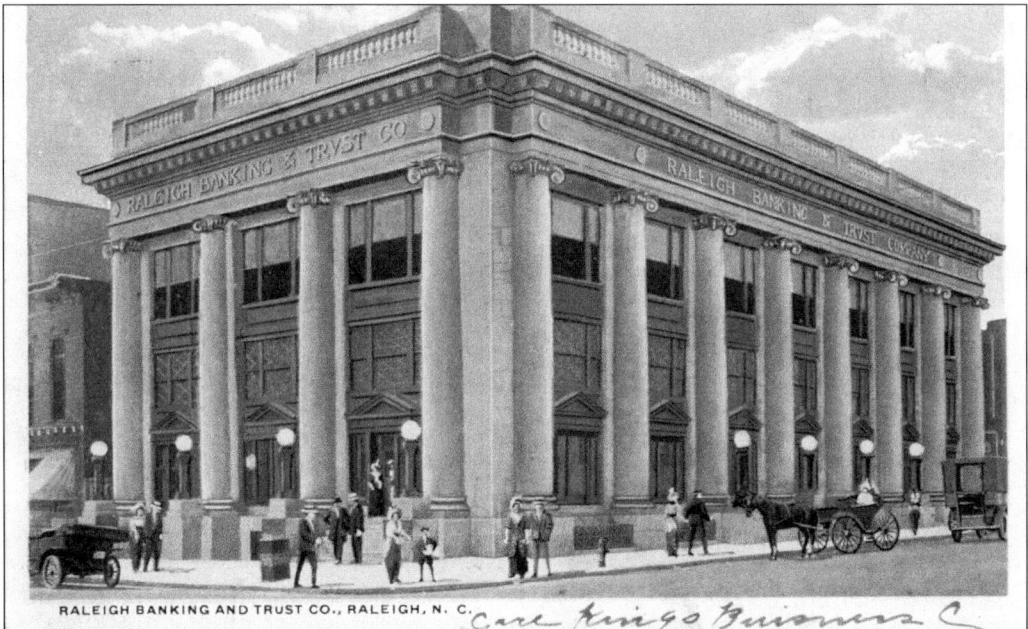

RALEIGH BANKING AND TRUST CO., RALEIGH, N. C.

The message on the back of this white border card proclaims, "Raleigh Banking and Trust Company is the oldest bank in Raleigh, being established in 1865. Active and Savings Accounts Invited." The building shown here, on the southwest corner of Fayetteville and Hargett Streets, was built in the 1880s. The foundation and steel framework were designed so that additional floors could be added at a later date. (Peggy Holliday.)

Eight stories were added in the 1920s to the Raleigh Banking and Trust Building. This building, of Neoclassical Revival architecture, is now known as the Raleigh Building and the upper floors are used for offices. (North Carolina Museum of History.)

The Odd Fellows Lodge built the I.O.O.F. Temple on the southeast corner of Hargett and Salisbury Streets in 1923–24. A printed message on the back advises, "ODD FELLOWS TEMPLE AND OFFICE BUILDING contains 110 offices. The Lodge Room is located on the ninth floor, with balcony on tenth." The building was recently renovated for office space.

31

Professional Bldg., Raleigh, N. C.

The Professional Building, a block to the west of the Odd Fellows Building, is on the southeast corner of Hargett and McDowell Streets. In this case the card's publisher reported, "Professional Building, erected in 1925 by Wachovia Bank & Trust Company, Trustee, an office building modern in every respect, built primarily for physicians, surgeons, dentists, and other professional men, but available to others." In the early 1980s this building also was renovated for office use.

LAWYERS BUILDING, RALEIGH, N. C.

The Lawyer Building is located across Salisbury Street to the west from the Wake County Courthouse. The building opened in 1924 and most of its occupants, as the name suggests, were lawyers. The State Theater, which opened as a vaudeville house and later became a movie theater, occupied most of the first floor for many years.

32

The Capital Club Building is located on the northeast corner of Salisbury and Martin Streets. The Capital Club was established in 1891 as a literary and social organization. This building is twelve stories high, made of brick, and was designed by Frank P. Milburn. The building is presently used for offices.

CAPITAL CLUB BUILDING RALEIGH N C   OA3657

CITIZEN NATIONAL BANK, RALEIGH, N. C.   111332

The Citizens National Bank opened this building at the northeast corner of Martin and Fayetteville Streets in 1912. The building later was used by the North Carolina National Bank and Trust Company and the Security National Bank. The building shown on the card was demolished in the 1960s to make room for the building presently occupied by First Citizens Bank.

COMMERCIAL NATIONAL BANK, RALEIGH, N. C.

The Commercial National Bank Building, with its ten stories, was the tallest building in Raleigh when it was completed in 1912. It was designed by Atlanta architect P. Thornton Marye, who also drew the plans for the 1911 Municipal Building and Memorial Auditorium.

In May of 1915, a gentleman billing himself as the "Human Fly" successfully climbed the outside of the Commercial National Bank Building. A local newspaper reported that this feat "elicited applause and loudly spoken admiration for his nerve." About a month later, the "Human Fly" fell 45 feet while trying to climb the South Carolina Capitol in Columbia. With the exception of several broken ribs, the "Human Fly" was not seriously injured.

The building was acquired by First Citizens Bank in 1930. On March 24, 1991, the building was once again in the news. At precisely 7:29 am, explosives were set off; in less than six seconds, the building was a pile of rubble and twisted steel!

The Busy Bee Café

225 SOUTH WILMINGTON STREET
RALEIGH, N.C.

RALEIGH'S POPULAR RESTAURANT

PRIVATE DINING ROOM FOR LADIES

MODERN EQUIPMENT···· POLITE, QUICK SERVICE

An ad that ran regularly in a Raleigh newspaper around 1915 invited customers to visit the Busy Bee Cafe. They promised, "Everything New, Perfectly Clean, Well Appointed, Guaranteed Satisfaction." The owners also boasted of a private dining room for ladies and offered meal tickets, which were popular at the time. A ticket for $1.15 cost $1, $2.30 was priced at $2, and the $3.50 ticket could be had for $3. Coffee, tea, milk, or buttermilk were free with each meal ordered. (Durwood Barbour.)

The Masonic Temple, later renamed the Alexander Building, is at 133 Fayetteville Street. Designed by South Carolina architect Charles Miller, it was the first reinforced-concrete building constructed in North Carolina. Completed in 1907, it is now on the National Register of Historic Places. The interior was completely renovated in the early 1980s.

MASONIC TEMPLE. RALEIGH. N. C.

add. LAYING OF "CORNER STONE,"
WEDNESDAY, OCTOBER 16, 1907.

RALEIGH N. C.
Olivia Raney
Library.

The three-story Olivia Raney Library was completed in 1900 on the corner of Hillsborough and Salisbury Streets. Space was provided for book stacks, a reading room, a smoking room for gentlemen, a reception room for ladies, an apartment for the librarian, and a music hall on the top floor. Money for the building and furnishings was donated by Richard B. Raney in memory of his wife, Olivia Cowper Raney.

Fire Station # 1, or Central Station, was completed in 1892 on West Morgan Street for the city's all-volunteer fire service. The first paid fire fighters joined a newly organized fire department in late 1912, at about the same time the first motorized equipment was added. The building shown above served as the department's headquarters until the late 1930s. This real photo view is believed to have been taken about 1919.

The Market, Raleigh, N. C.

The Market House stood on Fayetteville Street between Exchange Street and Market Place. Farmers in the early days used the first floor and adjacent Market Street to sell their produce. The police department and jail at one time were housed in the basement. Court was held on the second floor and the Mayor's Office was also located there. Opera performances were staged and later movies shown on the top floor. The Wachovia Bank Building presently occupies the site. (Durwood Barbour.)

Post Office Building, Raleigh, N.C.

The old Federal Building, known simply as the Post Office for most of its life, was completed in 1877 on the southwest corner of Fayetteville and Martin Streets. Now called the Century Post Office, the building has been renovated several times over the years. Major changes in appearance include the removal of the chimneys and the enlargement of the entrance.

County Court House, Raleigh, N.C.

The Wake County Courthouse was next door and to the south of the Post Office in the 300-block of Fayetteville Street. The Courthouse shown here was completed in 1835 and renovated in 1882. It is believed to have been the third Courthouse on this site.

A new Wake County Courthouse was completed in 1915 and served as the headquarters for county government until 1967. At that time it was replaced with the Courthouse that now occupies the site. Kings Business College is on the left and the Post Office on the right. Notice that the Post Office chimneys are gone in this view.

Raleigh's Municipal Building and Auditorium were located on Fayetteville Street and completed in 1911. In addition to the auditorium seating 5,000, the building housed the offices of city officials, the police headquarters, a courtroom, and the city jail. For nearly twenty years, most events of any consequence took place at the auditorium. Then, on October 24, 1930, fire destroyed the auditorium and the city offices suffered smoke and water damage. Although the auditorium was damaged beyond repair, the building continued to serve as City Hall for many years.

City officials did not waste time in replacing the old municipal auditorium. The Memorial Auditorium, constructed at the south end of Fayetteville Street on the site of the old Centennial School, was completed in 1932. The new facility could seat three thousand spectators and soon was a busy place hosting concerts, theatrical performances, the inauguration of governors, and the annual Debutante Ball.

Aunt Betsy Holmes and her Horseless Carriage, Raleigh, N. C.

Most postcards of early downtown Raleigh featured buildings and street views. Perhaps the most popular subject of postcard photographers was Aunt Betsy Holmes, shown being pulled around town with her bull, Joe. This view shows her at the corner of Edenton and Halifax Streets with the First Baptist Church in the background.

Uncle Bob.

Raleigh N.C. Sept 30 - 13

Cards of Uncle Bob are not as common as those of Aunt Betsy. The penciled message on the face of this card, postmarked September 30, 1913, states, "This is a familiar sight on the streets of Raleigh. Expect to start my return trip tomorrow." Although Aunt Betsy is always shown in a four-wheel buggy and Uncle Bob in a two-wheel cart, the motive power always seems to have been Joe, the bull. (Durwood Barbour.)

Some of Raleigh's oldest churches are located across from Capitol Square. The First Presbyterian Church was organized in 1816 and is on the southwest corner of Morgan and Salisbury Streets. The General Assembly met here after the first Capitol burned in 1831 and while the present Capitol was being built. The present sanctuary, shown here, was dedicated in September of 1900. The Raleigh Water Tower, to the west of the church, is on the right.

The First Baptist Church, located across from Capitol Square on the southwest corner of the intersection of Salisbury and Edenton Streets, was organized in 1812. The present church, first occupied in 1859, was designed by William Percival. Although many additions and renovations have occurred over the past century, the main structure still retains much of its original appearance.

Christ Church is located across Wilmington Street from the Capitol. The stone church shown here was the creation of Richard Upjohn. The main structure was consecrated in 1854 and the tower and steeple were added in 1861. The steeple is topped with a weather vane and chicken—some say this was the last chicken left in Raleigh when Yankee troops left the city.

The Church of the Good Shepherd was organized in 1874 by a group from Christ Church who were opposed to the practice of selling pews. Although the cornerstone of the church shown here was laid in 1899, the stone building was not completed until 1914. This late Gothic Revival structure was designed by C.E. Hartge, who also drew the plans for several other Raleigh buildings. The church is located on the southeast corner of the intersection of Hillsborough and McDowell Streets. (Peggy Holliday.)

The cornerstone of the Edenton Street Methodist Church is inscribed, "Organized 1811, Rebuilt 1841–1881–1951–1957." The church shown on this card was built in 1881; at that time the 184-foot steeple was the highest structure on the Raleigh skyline. The present Edenton Street Methodist Church was built after a fire destroyed the old church on July 28, 1956. The parsonage shown on this card was demolished in 1954 after a new parsonage was built.

Edenton Street Methodist is one of the largest churches in the North Carolina Conference, with a membership of over twenty-five hundred people. It has been the church home of governors, senators, and ambassadors, and has aided in the establishment of several other Methodist churches in Raleigh. (Ed Williams.)

This Private Mailing Card of the Epworth M.E. Church is one of the oldest-known postcards of Raleigh. It was printed on buff-colored stock using black ink. The church was located for most of its life on the corner of Halifax and Franklin Streets. Epworth Church merged with Central Methodist Church to form what is now Trinity Methodist Church on Bloodworth Street.

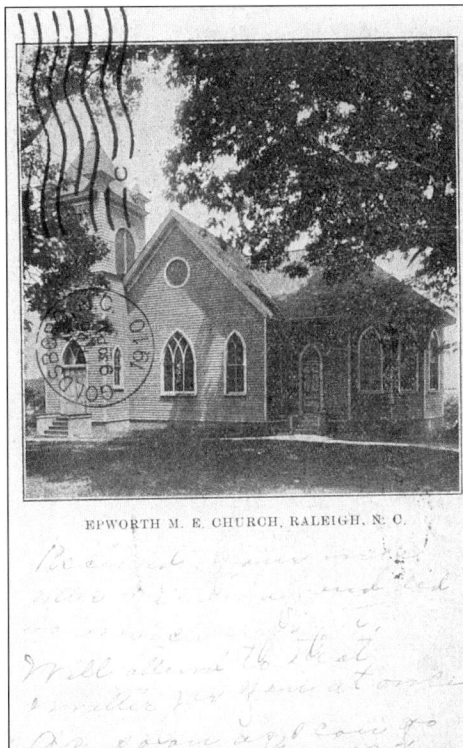

EPWORTH M. E. CHURCH, RALEIGH, N. C.

The New Baptist Tabernacle Church was organized in 1874 when some members of First Baptist Church felt the need for another church. The church moved in 1881 to its present location across from Moore Square on Person and Hargett Streets. The church went through some six remodelings and additions from 1881 to 1909. The divided back card shown here was postmarked April 20, 1911.

SIMMS' BARACA CLASS, TABERNACLE SUNDAY SCHOOL, RALEIGH, N.C.

National Motto.—"Young men at work for young men; all standing by the Bible and the Bible School."

Churches often used postcards as a means of attracting new members or as a gentle reminder to those whose attendance had slipped. Printed on the back of this card was a poem by Luther M. Tesh: "Boys, let's be a blessing, Always helping others. Remember those around us, Are simply our brothers; Can't we make them happy, And win them all to Christ, By pointing out the dangers, On the road to life? Young Men, Christ can use us; So let him do His will."

The Yarborough House, across Fayetteville Street from the Courthouse, was Raleigh's premier hotel for more than seventy-five years. Built in 1852, it served as a social center and also provided lodging for visitors. Several North Carolina governors called it home between 1865 and 1889. Lawmakers spent so much time here it often was called the "Second Capitol."

The hotel was renovated in 1904 and new wings added. Although this card bears no postmark, the note of "May 16, 1906" on the face of the card suggests the view was made shortly after the renovations and additions were completed. The Yarborough was destroyed by fire on July 3, 1928.

Postcards have been used by hotels to advertise their services for most of this century. Complimentary copies are placed in the rooms and the lobby for those who want to drop a line or two to the folks back home. This view was made after the hotel was renovated in 1904 and new wings added. As the message indicates, rooms without a bath were less expensive than those with one. Note the Yarborough had the European Plan, which means guests got three meals plus a room for $1–$3 a night!

The Hotel Arcade was located at 122 East Hargett Street. The advertisement on the back of the card reads, "Select family and tourist hotel. Running water in each room. Private dining rooms, with parlor for receptions. P. T. Hall, Prop." And for those who wanted to call ahead for a reservation, only a four-digit number was needed: "9146."

HOTEL ARCADE AND LOBBY. RALEIGH, N. C.

The main Meredith College building became the Mansion Park Hotel when Meredith moved to its new campus in West Raleigh. Located between the Capitol and the Governor's Mansion, the hotel had 122 rooms and 100 baths. It also served as the headquarters of the Carolina Motor Club (AAA). The message on this card, postmarked May 1, 1930, was typical postcard prose: "Hot as pepper sass on today's trip across 218 miles."

Numerous cards have been published showing the Hotel Sir Walter. "The only Hotel in Raleigh with circulating ice water in every room and an air-conditioned restaurant," is the way one card put it. The Sir Walter also boasted of having Turkish baths and its own laundry and garage. The building has been renovated and now contains apartments for senior citizens.

46

The Bland Hotel opened in 1912, just in time to house many of the delegates to the North Carolina Republican Convention. The hotel had seventy-two rooms with baths and eight without baths. The hotel's location at the northwest corner of Salisbury and Martin Streets made it convenient to the old train station and, in later years, to the bus station on Martin Street. Several businesses occupied space on the ground floor of the hotel over the years. Later renamed the Andrew Johnson Hotel, it closed for business in 1975. The message on the back of this card, postmarked November 10, 1930, reads in part, "We stayed over night in this hotel on our way down." The card was mailed from Saint Petersburg, Florida, to a gentlemen in Ocean City, Maryland.

The parlor of the Bland was not as large or fancy as the parlors of some of Raleigh's other hotels, but it appears comfortable and "homey." Wicker furniture, which was popular before the turn of the century, was still very much in use when this view was taken. Note how the electrical cord for the table lamp is attached to the light socket at the top of the picture. This divided back card was postmarked May 23, 1918.

The Hotel Carolina was located on the northeast corner of Hargett and Dawson Streets. The management hailed it as "Raleigh's Newest and Finest Hotel," with 250 rooms, each with a bath, radio, and electric fan. The Hotel Carolina was demolished in the late 1970s to make way for Raleigh's new Municipal Building.

HOTEL WILEY, RALEIGH, N. C.   (LOCATED IN RESIDENTIAL SECTION OF CITY).   107682

The Hotel Wiley occupied the building at the southeast corner of Morgan and West Streets that previously served the community as Wiley School. Both the school and the hotel were named in honor of Calvin Wiley, an educator who did for North Carolina many of the same things that Horace Mann did for Massachusetts. Mr. William Fowler, the father of one of the authors of this book, used to "carry" his son "B.T." to the barber shop in the Hotel Wiley. This was back when a haircut was 25¢!

Martin Street and Park Hotel. looking East. Raleigh, N. C.

A 1904 booklet published by the Raleigh Chamber of Commerce and Industry reported that Howell Cobb, the progressive proprietor of the Yarborough House, "has recently purchased the Park Hotel, a comparatively new hotel, of one hundred rooms, beautifully located on Nash Square." Cobb promised to remodel and convert it "into a hotel of the very best class, and cater to the best element of winter tourist travel."

RALEIGH HOTEL, SHOWING WEST MARTIN STREET, LOOKING EAST, RALEIGH, N. C.

The Park Hotel became the Hotel Raleigh. By comparing the postcards of the two hotels, you can see that awnings have been added, but that the trees are only a bit larger. The Hotel Raleigh boasted of offering "every comfort and convenience, including up-to-date elevator service." The hotel in its later years operated as the Park Central Hotel.

49

HOTEL RALEIGH.   RALEIGH. N. C.

Several interiors of the Hotel Raleigh were published and probably given to those who took advantage of the hotel's modern lodgings. Hotels back in those days had spacious lobbies, which were favorite meeting places for traveling salesmen and other guests. (Durwood Barbour.)

DINING ROOM, HOTEL RALEIGH
RALEIGH, N.C.

The dining room of the Hotel Raleigh, according to one source, could seat one hundred guests. The room's furnishings and the table settings suggest this was one of Raleigh's nicer places to eat. (Durwood Barbour.)

The Union Railroad Station, across from Nash Square, opened for business in 1892. Railroads serving Raleigh at the time were the Raleigh and Augusta Air-Line, the Raleigh and Gaston, and the North Carolina Railroad. The station was located on a spur off the main tracks, and the trains were backed into the station. Many traveled to and from the station via the street cars that ran down Dawson Street in front of the station. Train service to this station was discontinued in 1950 and later the building was remodeled for business and office use.

The Union Bus Station was located in the 200-block of West Morgan Street, which made it convenient to hotels, downtown businesses, and government offices. This linen card shows the station at the time it served all the major bus companies. The building contained a restaurant, newsstand, and snack bar, along with a spacious lobby. After Greyhound and Trailways built their separate stations, the property was acquired by the City of Raleigh. A parking deck, part of the Municipal Office Complex, now occupies the site.

The Raleigh Municipal Airport was located on South Wilmington Street (US Routes 70 and 401) and Tyron Road. The airport served most of the capital city's aviation needs from 1929 until after World War II, when all commercial flights moved to the present airport site midway between Raleigh and Durham. The message of this card, postmarked November 27, 1943, reads, "We all landed in Raleigh, N. C. last night. Leave for Georgia tomorrow morning and will cut cross country from there. Nice and warm down here. Nice airport here. Have army program. Write later."

The Capital Apartments, a five-story brick structure, was constructed in 1917 at 127 New Bern Avenue. This is one of Raleigh's earliest "high-rise" apartment buildings and features a U-shaped layout, which allows light and breezes to reach all the apartments. Only a block from Capitol Square, the conveniently located building still is used as an apartment complex.

The Young Men's Christian Association for years was located across from the Capitol on the northwest corner of Edenton and Wilmington Streets. When the "Y" outgrew these facilities, a new "Y" was built on Hillsborough Street not far from Pullen Park and North Carolina State University. Recently the new North Carolina Museum of History was constructed where the old YMCA once stood. Postmarked September 19, 1916, the card's message in part reads, "Hello there sister. I haven't seen you for so long. I don't know if you are living—dead—or married, so send me a card or something and let me know how you all are, as I am anxious to hear from old Frederick, Maryland."

Over the years the old Academy of Music, at the corner of Martin and Salisbury, hosted entertainers like Will Rogers, W.C. Fields, Ethel and John Barrymore, and as a special attraction, prize fighter Jim Corbett. The only known postcard of one of the attractions appearing at the Academy is this one of Blanche Ring and the Wall Street Girls. (Durwood Barbour.)

Andrew Jackson (1808–1875), the seventeenth President of the United States, was born in this small house, which at the time was located near where the Justice Building stands today. Over the years the house was moved three times before being located in the Mordecai Square Historical Park in 1981. President Jackson, who served from 1865 to 1869, was one of three presidents born in North Carolina. The other two were Andrew Johnson of Mecklenberg County, who served from 1829 to 1837, and James Polk from Union County, who served from 1845 to 1849. A statue was erected on Capitol Square in 1948 in honor of these three North Carolinians; it is located on the east side of the Capitol facing New Bern Avenue.

Several early Raleigh postcards featured views of the residences located near the Capitol and business district. The houses on the left were located immediately across Edenton Street from the Capitol. Today this site is occupied by the recently completed North Carolina Museum of History. Christ Church is on the right.

This card, postmarked in 1920, shows the residences in the 200-block of Blount Street, across from the Governor's Mansion. For many years Blount Street was "the" place to live and many of the city's most influential citizens had homes there. Most of this part of Raleigh is now occupied by state office buildings and parking lots.

Hillsboro Street, Raleigh, N. C.

This view of Hillsborough (spelled Hillsboro at one point) Street looks west from the Confederate Monument on Capitol Square. Most of the stately homes in this part of the city are gone, but the Sacred Heart Catholic Church, barely visible in the background, still stands at Hillsborough and McDowell. The church steeple on the right tops Edenton Methodist Church. Note the streetcar coming down Hillsborough Street on the double tracks, which turned south on Salisbury Street.

The Raney House was located at 102 Hillsborough Street, just across the street from Capitol Square. The house was built by Richard B. Raney, who also gave the funds for building the Olivia Raney Library. The house was eventually removed to make way for surface parking, which has also been the fate of several of the other beautiful old homes in the downtown area. (Durwood Barbour.)

The postcard caption identifies this as the "Home of Marshall DeLancey Haywood, Raleigh, N. C. Erected in 1854 by Dr. Richard B. Haywood on Part of Square Purchased by Sherwood Haywood in 1800." Dr. Richard Haywood, one of the city's leading citizens in the mid-1800s, was a graduate of the Jefferson Medical College in Philadelphia and served as president of the North Carolina Medical Society. He also served as a major in the Confederate Army. He was a member of the group whose duty it was to surrender Raleigh before the advance of Union troops.

Marshall DeLancey Haywood inherited the property and lived in the Haywood House at 127 East Edenton Street until his death in 1933. The house is still occupied by members of the Haywood family. (Durwood Barbour.)

Thomas Henry Briggs and James Dodd opened a small store at 220 Fayetteville Street in August of 1865. In 1874 a new building was constructed on the site and not long afterwards Dodd retired from the partnership. Since then Raleigh's oldest hardware store has been known as T.H. Briggs and Sons. Although the Briggs Hardware Store seems not to have been featured on a postcard, we do have a postcard of the Briggs family home on West Edenton. (North Carolina Museum of History.)

The Heck-Andrews house at 309 North Blount Street was completed about 1870 for Colonel and Mrs. Jonathan McGee Heck. This Second Empire-style house was among the first of Raleigh's mansions to be built after the Civil War. After Heck's death in 1894, the residence remained in his family until 1921, when it was sold to A.B. Andrews. The house was sold again in 1946 when Mr. Andrews died. Note there was snow on the ground when this c. 1920 photograph was taken. (Durwood Barbour.)

The Baptist University for Women opened in 1899 as Baptist Female University and was known by that name until 1904; in 1909 the institution took its present name of Meredith College. The impressive five-story main building was designed by architect G.A. Bauer, who also did the present Governor's Mansion. When Meredith moved from Blount Street to its new West Raleigh campus in late 1925, the building shown here became the Mansion Park Hotel. Later the building was purchased by the state to house the Commission for the Blind; it was taken down in 1967.

Raleigh, N. C. Faircloth Hall. Baptist University for Women.

Faircloth Hall opened in the fall of 1904 and with the additional space, enrollments jumped from the 279 to 354 students. In addition to bedrooms for ninety-six students, there were classrooms, practice rooms, and two "society halls" on the fourth floor. The building was sold to the YMCA when Meredith moved to its new campus in West Raleigh. Later the building became the McAlpin Hotel and in 1960 it was razed and replaced by the Heart of Raleigh Motel, which in turn was later taken down to make space for a parking lot for state government employees. (Peggy Holliday.)

Popular with collectors is an artist series of postcards by F. Earl Christy featuring college girls. With such cards not available for the smaller schools, an enterprising Meredith student used her own hand-colored card to tell a young man at nearby Wake Forest College that she couldn't come to Saturday's baseball game. (Bill Murphy.)

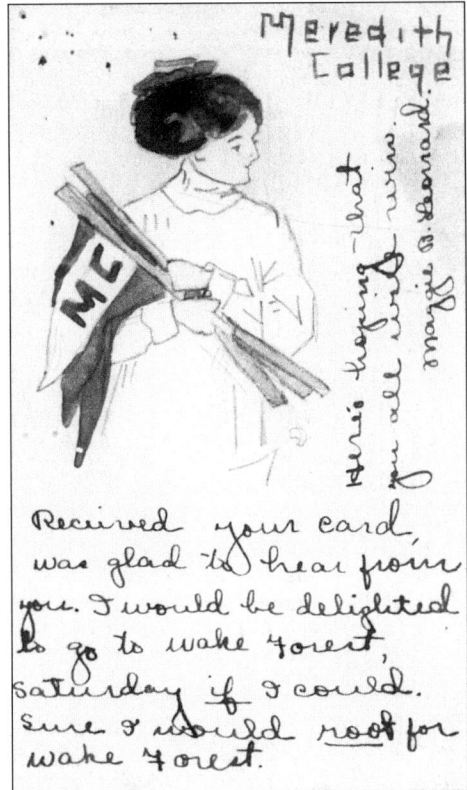

Meredith College

Here's hoping that you are still well. ...

Maggie B. Leonard

Received your card, was glad to hear from you. I would be delighted to go to wake forest, saturday if I could. Sure I would root for wake forest.

MEREDITH COLLEGE

Judging by the cars, this is a view of the campus shortly after Meredith moved to its present location in west Raleigh. Johnson Hall, the administration building, is on the right, and two of the dormitories are on the left.

Main Building, Agricultural and Mechanical Arts University, Raleigh, N.C.

The North Carolina College of Agriculture and Mechanical Arts opened in the fall of 1889. Main Building contained classrooms, faculty offices, barracks-like dormitory rooms, and the dining room with its adjacent kitchen. A&M College is now North Carolina State University, known worldwide for its programs in science and technology. Main Building, which was later named Holladay Hall in honor of A&M's first president, presently houses the offices of the chancellor and other campus administrators.

S.B. Coley's drawing made in 1911 shows the rapid growth of the campus during A&M's first twenty years. Most of these buildings are still in use, but Riddick Field in the upper left is now a parking lot.

This aerial view, postmarked 1937, shows the recently completed Memorial Tower, which honors the thirty-three alumni who lost their lives in World War I. At first glance you may conclude that the campus had not changed much from that shown in Coley's 1911 sketch. Wrong! The publisher superimposed the Memorial Tower over a photograph of the campus taken in 1920. The moral of the story is that information on postcards needs to be double-checked to ensure accuracy.

The NC State postcards in the book can be used as a guide for a walking tour of the older part of the campus. In the case of buildings, date of completion is given in parentheses.

Peele Hall (1928) is immediately to the west and north of Holladay Hall and across the street from the Memorial Tower. The Mechanical Building, housing metal and wood working shops, once occupied this site. The Admissions Office and the Graduate School are presently housed in Peele Hall.

This sepia card and several others of buildings at NC State were published individually and also in booklet form by the Albertype Company; they were sold individually and as a book by the Campus Student Supply Store.

Pullen Hall (1902) contained an auditorium seating eight hundred, dining hall space for five hundred, and a library to house the three thousand or so books the college owned when the building opened. On one occasion, students in protest of compulsory chapel attendance turned a "borrowed" bear loose in Pullen Hall. Needless to say, chapel was canceled until the bear was returned to its cage in nearby Pullen Park. Pullen Hall was destroyed by fire in 1965 and the site is presently a parking lot on the north side of Peele Hall. (Durwood Barbour.)

Primrose Hall (1896) is one of the smallest buildings on campus. Over the years it has been home to Horticulture, Civil Engineering, the YMCA, a campus bookstore, Economics, Modern Languages, ROTC, Geological Engineering, Personnel, and most recently, the Office of Campus Planning. As the caption on the card suggests, it was the home of the YMCA at the time this scene was photographed. The first textile building, Tompkins Hall, is in the rear. (Durwood Barbour.)

Tompkins Hall (1901), which resembles an old southern textile mill, was built to house the college's textile program. This view, postmarked February 2, 1908, is of the original Tompkins Hall, which was partially destroyed by fire in 1914. The tower was later modified and eventually the top part was removed. The animal grazing on the right may have added credence to A&M's reputation as a "cow college." (Durwood Barbour.)

Engineering Building.
Agricultural and Mechanical Art Institute,
Raleigh, N. C.

Winston Hall (1910) originally housed programs in engineering, but the majority of NCSU alumni remember Winston as the place where they took their English courses. Recently Winston and Tompkins were renovated and linked by new construction. This "Link Building" has been named Caldwell Hall in honor of late Chancellor John T. Caldwell.

Agricultural Building Agricultural and Mechanical Arts University Raleigh

Patterson Hall (1903) is up a small hill to the west of Winston and faces Hillsborough Street. It was the first building on this part of the campus, which became known as "Ag Hill." At the time Patterson opened, the State Fairgrounds were located across Hillsborough Street to the north.

Note the open area intersected with sidewalks in the lower part of this 1930s aerial view of the campus. Patterson Hall is the building on the left of the open area; going around counterclockwise are Polk Hall, the Animal Industries Building, Daniels Hall, and Withers Hall. Just to the left of Withers is Ricks Hall. Be sure also to note the smokestack, with "STATE COLLEGE" clearly visible to those who passed by the campus.

The Animal Industries Building (1912), a block to the south of Patterson, housed Animal Industries, Poultry, Entomology, and Zoology. The students on the campus tennis courts remind us that colleges always have been more than buildings and classes. Mann Hall was built on the site of the Animal Industries Building. The first nuclear reactor to be built on a college campus was constructed on the site of the tennis courts shown on this postcard. (Postcard Collection, Special Collections, North Carolina State University Libraries.)

Polk Hall (1926, with an addition in 1963) and several other newer buildings surround an open area officially designated as the University Plaza, but affectionately known by all Wolfpackers as the "Brick Yard." Polk is home to programs in Animal Science and Biochemistry. (Postcard Collection, Special Collections, North Carolina State University Libraries.)

Daniels Hall (1926) is located a short block to the east of Polk and houses engineering classrooms and laboratories. Daniels was named in honor of Josephus Daniels, an editor of Raleigh's *News and Observer* and secretary of the navy in Woodrow Wilson's cabinet.

Note the single car parked in front of the building. With today's parking problems, the only time this happens now is when the street is being repaired.

Back up the street to the north of Daniels Hall is Ricks Hall (1922). Note that the last three buildings visited—as well as several others on the campus—were built in the 1920s, when enrollments were increasing and money was relatively plentiful. Ricks Hall is the headquarters for the Agricultural Extension Service, which has a network of extension agents in each of the state's one hundred counties.

In this 1930s view of Ceres Court looking north, a corner of Polk Hall is visible on the left. Other buildings, from left to right, are: Patterson Hall, Ricks Hall, Withers Hall, and part of Daniels Hall. The south end of Ceres Court is now occupied by Burlington Nuclear Laboratories, where the first nuclear reactor on a college campus was placed in operation on September 5, 1953. The M.E. Gardner Arboretum is now located on the northern part of the court.

Around the corner and to the east of Ricks Hall is the 1911 Building (1909). This view shows the building shortly after it opened; at the time it was one of the largest dormitories in the South. Later additions on both ends added space for another one hundred-plus students. Some say the building was built in 1911 and officials never got around to giving it another name. This is not the case. The building was named in honor of the senior class of 1911, which in its sophomore year officially banned the hazing of freshmen.

71

Page Hall (1922), across the street to the east from the 1911 Building, originally housed Mechanical Engineering. It now is the home of the administrative offices of the College of Engineering, the largest college at NCSU. The old German cannon, which for years commanded the best view of the Court of Carolina, was once found on the roof of Watauga Dormitory. Some enterprising engineering students were the prime suspects. Unlike the unknown identity of the campus pranksters, the eventual fate of the cannon is no secret—it was a victim of a scrap metal drive in the early days of World War II. (Postcard Collection, Special Collections, North Carolina State University Libraries.)

As the student body grew, dining facilities were moved from the Main Building (Holladay Hall) to Watauga Hall, and then to Pullen Hall. Leazar Hall (1912) served as the main campus dining facility until the early 1960s. Located on the south side of the Court of Carolina, Leazar faces the backside of Watauga. The Dairy Records Center, Design School laboratories, and computer laboratories presently occupy most of the building.

Watauga Hall (1896) was constructed as a dormitory and dining facility. After a fire destroyed the first building in 1901, the second Watauga Hall (shown here) was built a year or so later. Watauga became the first dormitory for women in 1964 and in 1985, after being renovated, became a dorm for graduate students. In addition to a cannon on the roof thought to have been placed there by engineering students, a cow was once found wandering around one of the upper floors. This time the agriculture students were blamed.

The Student Infirmary (1897) was located just south of Holladay Hall facing Pullen Road. Watauga Hall is visible in the right rear of the view. A major part of the old Student Infirmary has survived as the southern portion of the Alumni Building. An unknown person in Tuscarora, North Carolina, mailed this particular card on September 7, 1910, to a gentleman who was staying at a hotel in Goldsboro. (Postcard Collection, Special Collections, North Carolina State University Libraries.)

The original D.H. Hill Library (1926) provided space for the growing student body and collection of books and serials. Since Hill Library's move in the 1950s to its present location on the Brick Yard, the building has been occupied by the School of Design. It was renamed Brooks Hall in 1956.

This real photo postcard shows Syme Dorm (1916), originally called South Dorm, and the YMCA (1911). Basketball came to the campus though the influence of the "Y" shortly after its new building opened—before then basketball had been considered a "girls sport." The "Y," later renamed the King Religious Center, was taken down to make room for the Brooks Hall expansion. (Postcard Collection, Special Collections, North Carolina State University Libraries.)

A. & M. College Buildings, Raleigh, N. C.

217198

From right to left in this view of the campus from near Pullen Road and the railroad tracks are: Tompkins Hall (with the tower), Winston Hall, the 1911 Building, Patterson Hall, and the campus water tower. The campus power plant and Riddick field are in the foreground; visible in the distance between Tompkins Hall and Winston Hall is the grandstand at the State Fairgrounds.

Raleigh, N. C.—16

Riddick Field was used not only for football and baseball, but for physical education classes and a place to drill ROTC students. The upper view, believed to have been made in about 1923, shows a field covered with ROTC students and a small band lined up on left. In the lower view, the base of Memorial Tower is on the right and Pullen Hall is behind the tree just to the left of center.

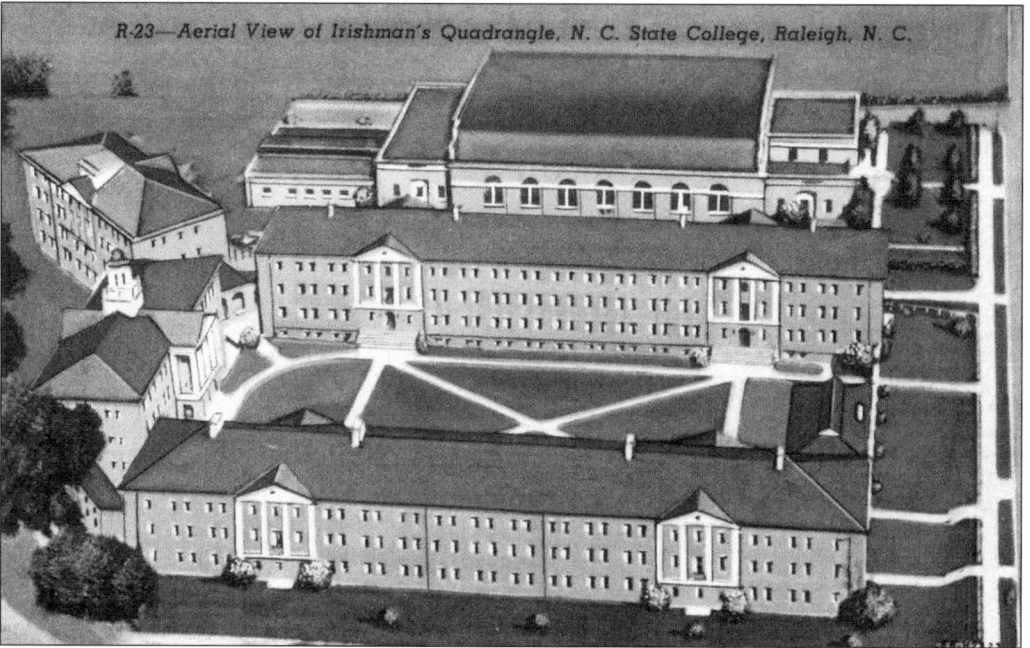

R-23—Aerial View of Irishman's Quadrangle, N. C. State College, Raleigh, N. C.

Among the first permanent buildings south of the railroad tracks were a dormitory complex and the Frank Thompson Gymnasium (1925), shown in the rear of this 1940s view. Starting in the foreground and going around the quadrangle clockwise are Bagwell Hall (1924), Berry Hall (1939), Clark Hall (1939), and Becton Hall (1939). Clark Hall is now home to the College Infirmary; the other buildings are still used as dormitories.

At one time the dormitories at NC State were numbered, but later they were renamed in honor of faculty, alumni, and famous North Carolinians. Seventh Dormitory (1924), facing Pullen Road, was the first dorm built south of the railroad tracks. It was renamed Bagwell Hall in honor of Eugene C. Bagwell, a 1904 civil engineering graduate of the college who became president of the Seaboard Airline Railroad.

Most of the buildings shown in this early 1940s view of the campus have been illustrated by individual postcards in this book. Exceptions include Welch Dorm (1920), facing Pullen Road and north of the railroad track on the right side of this card, and Gold Dorm (1920), immediately to the north of Welch. Both these buildings are still in use as student residences.

When the Frank Thompson Gymnasium opened in 1925, basketball and other indoor sports got a big boost. Named after a engineering student who excelled in several sports and who was killed in France in 1918, the Frank Thompson Gym was home to Wolfpack basketball until Reynolds Coliseum was completed in 1949. The building now houses the Frank Thompson Theater, with the University Craft Center on the lower floor.

77

Football
A. & M. COLLEGE vs. WEST VIRGINIA UNIVERSITY
THURSDAY, OCTOBER 22

THIS GAME IS ON THURSDAY OF FAIR WEEK, AND IS THE BIGGEST GAME THAT WILL BE PLAYED IN THE STATE THIS SEASON. YOU CANNOT AFFORD TO MISS THIS GAME

PLAYERS

Anthony, O. S.	Medlock, F. H.
Artz, J. W.	Nooe, D. B.
Bonner, J. S.	Ormand, M. F.
Cook, C. C.	Park, C.
Cook, C. E.	Plyler, R. A.
Cobbitt, W. T.	Proffitt, C. C.
Champion, J. V.	Ramsaur, M. S.
Cross, W. B.	Rand, P. R.
Craven, H. P.	Riddick, W. W.
Davis, R. V.	Rogers, W. H.
Ebron, J. D.	Rowe, L. M.
Evans, W. J.	Seifert, C. O.
Fowler, M. C.	Simmons, P. T.
Gant, R.	Stowe, F. T.
Hinson, M. T.	Temple, B.
Hodgin, W. H.	Tenny, P. G.
Johnson, W. M.	Townsend, W. T.
Lindsay, R. O.	Turner, M. B.
McDougal, J. E.	VanBrocklin, C. E.
Malone, C. B.	Winston, H. E.
Mason, J. H.	Young, R. C.

A. & M. Football Squad

DR. J. E. HEGARTY - - - - - Coach   B. W. SETZER - - - - - - Manager
MIKE MARTIN - - - - - - Trainer   R. A. PLYLER - - - - - Captain
C. D. BRITTAIN and R. P. HILL, Assistant Managers

Postcards were once used to advertise NC State football games and in this case the 1914 contest between West Virginia University and A&M College, as NCSU was known as at the time. A local newspaper reported that "the game was played before a crowd of about 2,000 gridiron enthusiasts, among which ladies were very much in evidence." Attendance probably was helped with the North Carolina State Fair going on across Hillsborough Street from the campus. Coached by Dr. J.E. Hegarty and captained by R.A. Plyler, the A&M Techs won, 26–13!

OUR TEAM, A. & M. COLLEGE, WEST RALEIGH, N. C.

Although most campus postcards featured buildings, this one, postmarked in 1906, captured A&M's team lined up for the big play. The message written on the front adds to its interest: "Dear N— Here I am at the depot my train 1 hour late Had a nice time last night. Please excuse me for saying what I did. But I had to, don't mention it. Scottie." Wonder what he told the person to whom the card was sent? (Steve Massengill.)

Peace Institute, Raleigh, N. C.

Early postcards of Peace Institute feature the main building, with four white columns and balconies. Peace Institute was chartered in 1857, but the Civil War broke out before classes began. The structure shown here was used as a Confederate hospital during the war and later provided all the facilities needed by the students attending this Presbyterian school for girls. (Beth Crabtree Papers, Special Collections, North Carolina State University Libraries.)

Peace Institute, which later became Peace College, was named for William Peace, a prominent Raleigh merchant who gave $10,000 and 8 acres of land a few blocks north of the Capitol for the establishment of a female seminary. The institution has grown over the years, as shown by this view of the campus in the 1930s. Peace, like Saint Mary's just a few blocks away, admits only women. (Beth Crabtree Papers, Special Collections, North Carolina State University Libraries.)

Saint Augustine's Normal and Collegiate Institute, now Saint Augustine's College, was chartered in 1867 and the first classes were held the next year. The first major building was the four-story red brick Lyman Building, which at the time of its construction in 1884 housed the classrooms, offices, chapel, and men's quarters.

Saint Augustine's second building in the point of age was a beautiful stone chapel, built in 1896 with the aid of student labor. The quarrymaster and mason was the future Bishop Delany. The chapel contains memorial windows honoring the founders and early workers at the college. (Durwood Barbour.)

Built by students

As the handwritten message on the face of this early card indicates, Taylor Hall and Benson Library also were built by the students. The chapel, Taylor Hall, and Benson Library face Oakwood Avenue near the Main Gates to the campus and still are in use by the college. (Durwood Barbour.)

Saint Augustine's Saint Agnes Hospital was established in 1896 for the care of blacks and as a center for training nurses. A fire damaged much of the hospital in 1904, but the following year construction began on a new building, which was completed in 1909. The hospital operated until the 1940s, when it separated from the college to become a clinic. The clinic closed at about the time the Wake County Medical Center on New Bern Avenue opened in 1961. Dr. Hayden, a medical missionary, was superintendent of the hospital.

The message on the front of the card continues on the back, " . . . of the lesson was the Gift of Self. The lesson for this year will be Prayer. A small offering will be taken up each year or sent to Miss Mosley as a thanks offering (any amount). Wishing you great success." The card was signed, Daisy Belle Birdsall, postmarked June 20, 1914, and sent to a lady in Carthage, North Carolina.

Dr. Hayden, St. Agnes Hospital,
St. Augustine's School, Raleigh, N. C.

Saint Mary's, Raleigh's oldest college, opened its doors in May 1842. Raleigh's first school for young ladies occupied the campus of the defunct Episcopal School of North Carolina, which had opened eight years earlier a few blocks west of the Capitol on Hillsborough Street. Saint Mary's prospered and, unlike many other southern schools, remained open during the Civil War. Guests during the war included Mildred Lee, daughter of Robert E. Lee, and Mrs. Jefferson

St. Mary's School, Raleigh, N. C.

West Rock, the second oldest building on campus, was completed in early 1835. Like East Rock, which was constructed a year earlier, West Rock was built of blocks of stone rejected by masons building the new Capitol a few blocks to the East. West Rock has served as a dormitory for most of its lifetime and still serves that function. Although renovated several times, the rooms in West Rock are basically the same as when students lived there more than a half dozen generations ago. (Manuscript Collection, Duke University.)

Davis along with the three Davis children.

In this double postcard view of the campus in the early 1900s, students pose before Saint Mary's major buildings at the time. From left to right can be seen the rectory, the chapel, West Rock, Smedes Hall, East Rock, the Arts Building, and Pittman Auditorium.

Raleigh newspapers in the early 1900s frequently reported the Yarborough House and other hotels as being packed with visitors who had come south to enjoy Raleigh's mild climate. The chamber of commerce probably did not appreciate this snow scene at Saint Mary's, even though it was pointed out that such storms are infrequent. (Durwood Barbour.)

Shaw University was founded in 1865 "to provide instruction in the Bible in order that freed men might gain the knowledge necessary to establish churches though out the region." Two years later, in 1867, the school consisted of "three buildings, two of which were simple cabins." By the early 1900s, Shaw had grown to a campus of several buildings, three of which are in this view from Wilmington Street.

The Shaw Building, built in 1872, was the institution's first major building. Described as "the most capricious school building in North Carolina," it provided space for classrooms, a library, services, and lodging for male students. Shaw Hall was converted to a dormitory for women in 1944 and razed in 1967, just five years short of its 100th birthday. (Durwood Barbour.)

Estey Hall, the second building to be erected on the Shaw campus, housed the seventy women who were admitted to the new Female Department in 1874. Believed to be the first building used for the higher education of black women in the United States, Estey Hall is listed on the National Register of Historical Places. The building is being restored and will contain an auditorium, exhibit center, and meeting rooms.

The Leonard Building (left), completed in 1881, housed a medical school "to train Christian physicians to serve the health needs of the Negro Race." Shaw's first hospital, which opened in 1885, was replaced in 1912 by the brick structure shown on the right. The handwritten message on the back of the card, postmarked April 26, 1912, reads, "Does it look natural. Prof. E. designed and constructed it. Wish you could see it. Annie."

Raleigh High School, three years old at the time, moved into its new home on West Morgan Street in 1908. The modern facility contained eight classrooms, an auditorium, and a spacious basement. Next door to the school was Raleigh's Water Tower, which today is the home of the North Carolina Chapter of the American Institute of Architects. The high school building burned and was taken down in 1932. (Durwood Barbour.)

The original Washington School was a two-story frame structure erected in 1869 on the 100-block of West South Street. A new building, shown here, opened in the fall of 1924 on Fayetteville Street and housed both an elementary school and a high school for black students. Washington School is now a magnet elementary school for gifted and talented students. (Ed Williams.)

HUGH MORSON HIGH SCHOOL, RALEIGH, NORTH CAROLINA   R-12

Built at a cost of $500,000 dollars on a 4-acre site two blocks east of the Capitol, Hugh Morson High School opened in the fall of 1925. Named after the first principal of Raleigh High School, the Morson School served as a high school for thirty years and for another ten as a junior high school. The site was cleared in 1965 to make room for a new Post Office and Federal Building.

Raleigh got another high school when Needham Broughton opened in 1929 on Saint Mary's Street. The building was designed by local architect William Henley Deitrick, built of native stone, and named in honor of a Raleigh businessman and champion of better schools. Broughton is the city's oldest school still being used as a high school. The photographer, Bayard Wootten, is well known for her many views of North Carolina.

In the case of elementary schools, postcard publishers seem to have favored photos of students over those of buildings. This real photo postcard was mailed March 25, 1911, some three years before the original Murphey School on North Person Street was destroyed by fire. The second Murphey School built on the site was recently converted into apartments for the elderly.

The photographer taking these postcard views had an ingenious method for labeling the cards. It only took a few seconds to write the grade level and the name of the school and town on a small chalkboard, thus avoiding any mix-ups keeping track of the negatives. The biggest problem probably was deciding who would hold the sign.

The King's Business Colleges of Raleigh and Charlotte were founded in 1901 and headquartered in Raleigh. Several courses of study were offered, including "bookkeeping, shorthand, typewriting, penmanship, and also secretarial, banking, and machine bookkeeping work."

Five
Around the City

Numerous government buildings, hospitals, and recreational areas were located away from the downtown area and some at the time were outside the city limits. Postcards allow us a peek of what early Raleigh was like then and show us some of the ways the city has changed.

The State Hospital for the Insane opened in March of 1856 with eleven patients. The 726-foot-long central building was designed by Alexander J. Davis, the architect for the Capitol building. Long known as Dix Hill, this Raleigh landmark was named Dorothea Dix Hospital in honor of Miss Dix, who came to Raleigh in 1848 to urge the General Assembly to establish a state hospital for the mentally ill.

John Rex, a Raleigh merchant, provided money and land in 1839 for the establishment of a hospital. It was not until 1893, however, that his dream became a reality. At that time a financially troubled hospital was purchased from the Episcopal Church and renamed Rex Hospital. About fifteen years later a new hospital, shown here, was constructed on South Street.

Rex Hospital moved to a new, larger building on Saint Mary's Street in 1937. Several additions over the years greatly increased the size of the building shown on this card. With the need for additional space and more modern facilities in the 1970s, it was time to move again. Rex Hospital occupied its new home on Lake Boone Trail in 1980 and the old hospital was sold to the state to house the North Carolina Employment Securities Commission.

Mary Elizabeth Hospital opened in January of 1914 in a residence on the southeast corner of Halifax and Peace Streets. This privately owned hospital had only a dozen or so beds. In 1920 Mary Elizabeth moved to its new building, with forty-nine beds, at 1100 Wake Forest Road. This hospital closed in 1978, at which time the last five patients were moved to a recently completed Mary Elizabeth Hospital (now called Raleigh Community Hospital) farther out on Wake Forest Road. (Durwood Barbour.)

The Methodist Orphanage, later called the Methodist Home For Children, opened in 1900 on a 110-acre site bounded by Glenwood Avenue on the east and Saint Mary's on the west. The first major building on the campus was the Jenkins Building (shown here). At one time the Methodist Orphanage operated both an elementary school and a high school. Changes at the Orphanage beginning in the 1950s involved sending high school students to nearby Broughton. When the Orphanage closed, most of the land was sold to the city and county, with the remainder to real estate developers.

The State School for the Blind, now known as the Governor Morehead School in honor of Governor John Motley Morehead, moved to a spacious new campus on Ashe Avenue in West Raleigh in 1923. Among the original buildings was a gymnasium and swimming pool, now called the John E. Ray Gymnasium, which is where Governor Morehead students still take their physical education classes.

The Wake County Home for the Poor moved into this building on Whitaker Mill Road when it was completed in late 1915. The residents, at least those who were able, worked in the extensive gardens behind the home. The institution, like other county homes across the country, was expected to grow most of its own food. The building is now used as a Senior Citizens Center. (Durwood Barbour.)

The Confederate Soldiers Home was located a mile east of the Capitol near the present site of the Motor Vehicles Building. According to a historical marker on the corner of New Bern Avenue and Tarboro Road, the home operated from 1891 until 1933. Maps at the turn of century show several buildings making up the complex.

In the summer of 1892, shortly after the soldiers home opened, twenty-six veterans went to an encampment at Wrightsville Beach, near Wilmington. When interviewed about the trip, one of the old soldiers told a Raleigh newspaper that they had a good time. Then he added, "God Bless the Women of Wilmington; we will never forget them."

The Women's Club of Raleigh was organized in 1904 with its purpose being "the intellectual, philanthropic, social and domestic betterment of the City." The first meetings were held in the Olivia Raney Library. The building shown here was completed on Hillsborough Street in about 1915. It was sold in 1966 and taken down to make room for a high-rise Holiday Inn.

Lassiters Mill. Flour, Meal and Feed. Raleigh, N. C.

Lassiters Mill was located on Crabtree Creek in northwest Raleigh. The message printed on the back of the card reads:

"Lassiters water ground meal made of highest grade Corn, and well cleaned, contains no "Pelagra". Lassiters water ground Flour is made of best Wheat. It is not CHALK WHITE. It is CREAM WHITE; noted for Purity and designed for Health. Contains no Appendicitis and only requires one-half the usual amount of SODA. 'If you use LASSITERS MEAL be sure to try LASSITERS FLOUR.' " (Durwood Barbour.)

The Raleigh Country Club was incorporated in May of 1910 and 400 acres of land were purchased on what is now Glenwood Avenue. About half of the land was developed as a golf course and the remainder sold for other purposes. The name of the club was changed to the Carolina Country Club in 1918. The clubhouse shown here opened in about 1911 and was destroyed by fire on Labor Day, 1919.

CAROLINA COUNTRY CLUB. RALEIGH, N. C.

A second clubhouse opened in 1921. A fire broke out in this building during a severe snowstorm in the early morning of February 1, 1948. The building was completely destroyed; the club manager and four other family members lost their lives in the disaster. (Beth Crabtree Papers, Special Collections, North Carolina State University Libraries.)

Bloomsbury Park opened on July 4, 1912, in the northwestern part of the city near Lassiters Mill and the Carolina Country Club. Bloomsbury was a trolley park, with park visitors taking the Glenwood Avenue line to a station near the park entrance. With over eight thousand light bulbs decorating the park, Bloomsbury also was called "Electric Park."

Shortly after the park opened, a watchman decided to take a ride on the roller coaster one night to cool off. *Billboard* described what happened next: "The employee, when everybody had gone home, the story goes, took the car, reared back and turned on the 'juice.' The car climbed to the modest grade and passed nicely to the end of the track. But the man who puts on the brakes was not there. It reached the long climb again and up it went to the pinnacle the second time. The same circular course was continued and it then dawned upon the watchman that he was in for an all night's ride. Two o'clock, three, four, five, six, seven, eight, nine, ten, did he ride, when mercy came at last. The hands were then at work and he was saved."

The watchman reportedly got sick every time he looked at the roller coaster and eventually had to seek other employment. (North Carolina Department of Cultural Resources, Division of Archives and History.)

Attractions at the park included a carousel, penny arcade, boats on a small lake, and a dance hall. The park's patrons expected free entertainment and in 1915 Professor S. Battiato's Florentine Concert Band of fifteen pieces furnished the latest instrumental music. The same year *Billboard* reported that "the dancing end of the park has not been forgotten, as the dance pavilion will have a first-class instructor in the person of Prof. Sanchez Rountree, of Buenos Aires, S.A. Under his guiding hand the latest steps will be as popular and as well executed in a short time as it will be possible to do them."

The Dentzel carousel, at 5¢ a ride, was a favorite. However, Bloomsbury Park closed after only a few years of operation and the carousel was placed in storage. The carousel and the structure in which it was housed were eventually moved to Pullen Park. There you can still climb aboard a horse, cat, lion, giraffe, or one of the other magnificent steeds that once entertained visitors at Bloomsbury, but it now costs 60¢. Nevertheless, the carousel is a favorite and attracts visitors and carousel enthusiasts from all over the country.

THE FOUNTAIN.

THE BEAR PITS.

THE LILLY POND.

As Richard Stanhope Pullen walked ahead, employees plowed a furrow across the farm that he purchased in 1887. This furrow marked the boundary between the parcels that he donated to the City of Raleigh and state government, which were to become Pullen Park, and the College of Agricultural and Mechanical Arts. One of the park's early attractions was a small zoo, which began with the purchase of a pair of raccoons at the old city market. Later, bears, coyotes, foxes, ducks, and other animals were added.

Pullen Park's first swimming pool in 1890 was built entirely of wood. According to one report, the bathers for the first several years were all male and didn't bother to wear swimming suits. Later, one day a week was set aside for the "fair sex." The pool was enlarged and rebuilt with concrete in 1907. It was replaced with a picnic area when a new Aquatic Center opened a block to the north just off Ashe Avenue. In addition to the Aquatic Center, the carousel, miniature train, and paddle boats are popular attractions at Pullen Park.

WELCOME!

North Carolina State Fair and Home-Coming Jubilee

A JEFFERSON STANDARD POLICY IS A DECLARATION OF INDEPENDENCE FOR THE FAMILY

Compliments of the

Jefferson Standard Life Insurance Company

State fairs in North Carolina, beginning in 1853, entertained locals and out-of-towners alike on a 16-acre site about a dozen blocks east and a bit south of the Capitol. In 1873, the fair moved to a larger site on the north side of Hillsboro Road, across from what later was to become the A&M campus. The fair operated there though the 1925 season; there were no State Fairs in 1926 and 1927. The fair moved again in 1928, this time to its present location on Blue Ridge Road in West Raleigh.

E. F; McRae, Pres.   Jos. E. Pogue, Sec'y
53rd GREAT N. C. STATE FAIR
RALEIGH, N. C.   OCT. 14-19, 1912

A. T.   &   S F.   R Y.   2010.

Although the North Carolina State Fair operated during the Golden Age of Postcards in the early 1900s, few postcard views of the fair are known to exist. Advertising postcards, however, promoted the fair. Cards with exaggerated fruit, vegetables, and animals were not uncommon and today are prized collectibles. (North Carolina Collection, University of North Carolina Library at Chapel Hill.)

The cotton exhibit at the 1912 North Carolina State Fair on this rare real photo card is identified as being entered by W.A. Simpkins of Raleigh, North Carolina. In the lower left corner the person making the card added, "I REFUSED $10 FOR THIS STALL. OFFERED BY S. J. BETTS. N. C. STATE FAIR 1912."

Several of the prize winners in the cotton category at the 1912 North Carolina State Fair were exhibited by W.A. Simpkins. Note how the whole plants were exhibited, including some with leaves. Since the fair was held in October, it was possible to harvest these prize-winning plants from the field and bring them immediately to the fair.

Raleigh radio station WPTF, one of the pioneer stations in the United States, received its license on October 25, 1924. First known as WFQU and later as WRCO, the station was purchased in 1927 by the Durham Life Insurance Company. The call letters were later changed to WPTF (We Protect the Family). In the station's early days, live entertainment was featured, including the Lone Star Quartet shown on this card.

Raleigh television viewers back in the 1950s tuned in to WNAO, the capital city's CBS affiliate. The station's call letters were taken from Raleigh's morning newspaper, *The News and Observer*, which locals still refer to as the "N and O." During late 1956 and all of 1957, the station's studio (shown here) was located at 2128 Western Boulevard, on a triangular plot just across Ashe Avenue from the main entrance to Pullen Park. The building was also home to the Bon-Air and Caryle nightclubs and the Town and County Furniture Store. A convenience store presently occupies the site.

A TOURIST HOME OF SOUTHERN CHARM
Mrs. R. H. McKinney, Hostess
1209 Wake Forest Road ◊ U. S. No. 1
Raleigh, N. C.

Highway U.S. 1, which runs through Raleigh, stretches from Northern Maine to Key West, Florida. As the popularity of automobile travel increased, houses along the way were converted into tourist homes and many used postcards to advertise their accommodations. This tourist home was operated by Mrs. L.H. McKinney on the north edge of Raleigh's residential district.

WOOTEN'S HOMETEL
567 N. Person St., On U. S. Route 1
Raleigh, N. C.

Closer to downtown was Wooten's Hometel at 567 North Person Street. The message on the back of the card promised large, clean, cozy rooms. Cafe service was available daily, with delicious hot southern chicken and steak dinners. Just think, had the name caught on, today we might have "hometels" rather than "motels."

According to the Raleigh City Directories, Wooten's Hometel became Johnson's Hometel about 1936. Johnson's Hometel only operated for about five or six years, at which time the building reverted to residential use. In addition to the reasonable rates, southern home-cooked meals, and good beds offered by Wooten's Hometel, the Johnson's added the offer of a free garage.

Maple's Tourist Home was located at 216 North Person Street, near where the North Carolina Medical Society Building stands today. A guest used this card in 1945 to write home, "Arrived in Raleigh at 6:45 PM. Drove 577 miles. So far I have had a wonderful trip. This is where I am staying tonight. The people are so nice to me. I sure do like this country."

103

Just one block over from Maple's Tourist Home on Person Street was Mrs. J.C. Chamblee's Tourist Home at 227 North Blount Street. The Chamblee Home was in the block now occupied by the Archives and History Building and the North Carolina Records Building. A guest on the way to Florida from Massachusetts used this card in November of 1936 to say, "We stayed here last night and a lovely place and we have had nice weather and much warmer."

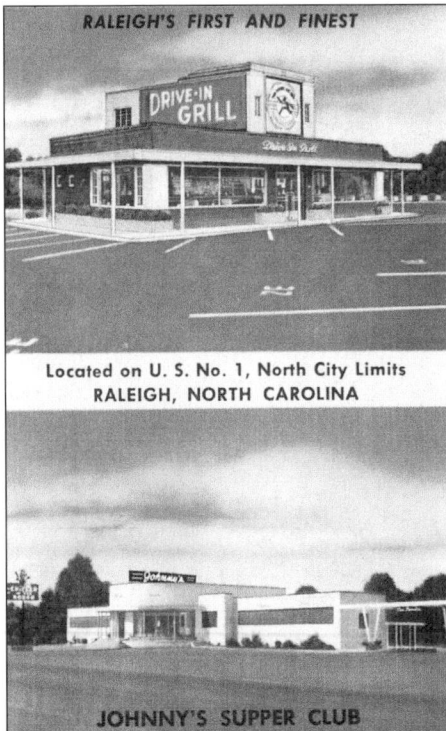

RALEIGH'S FIRST AND FINEST

DRIVE-IN GRILL

Located on U. S. No. 1, North City Limits
RALEIGH, NORTH CAROLINA

JOHNNY'S SUPPER CLUB

One of the capital city's first drive-in restaurants was Johnny's Drive-In Grill in the 1600-block of Capital Boulevard. Look carefully and you can see the numbers on the parking spaces, which helped attendants to keep the orders straight. The Pigeon Creek Restaurant presently occupies the building. Located nearby was Johnny's Supper Club; the Capital Inn is now located on the site of one of Raleigh's early nightclubs.

Six

Raleigh's Neighbors in Wake County

Until recently Wake County has been largely rural, with a smattering of small towns and crossroads country stores. Postcard views of Wake County communities include main streets, schools, churches, hotels, prominent homes, tourist attractions. and, in one case, a college. Following three introductory cards, the others are in alphabetical order, starting with Apex and ending with Zebulon. (Willard Jones.)

Cotton was once as much a part of the South as yams, black-eyed peas, and country ham. Postcard publishers capitalized on this stereotype and produced hundreds of views of cotton being harvested, usually by blacks. This card, an undivided back published about 1910, shows a scene near Raleigh while cotton was still an important crop in Wake County. By the time linen cards appeared in the 1930s, the production of cotton in the area was on the decline; however, during the last ten years, cotton has made an impressive comeback in eastern North Carolina. (Willard Jones.)

Tobacco is king in North Carolina and each year farmers in Wake County plant hundreds of acres. The bottom leaves are pulled first and hauled to drying barns to be cured. In this view made in the 1930s, a mule pulls a sled and the four young workers shown have the back-breaking job of selecting the leaves ready for harvest.

106

MAIN STREET
Apex, N. C.

The town of Apex, about a dozen miles southwest of Raleigh, was incorporated in 1873. A survey team had earlier given the community its name; Apex is the highest point on the railroad running from Richmond, Virginia, to Hamlet, North Carolina. Apex remained a small town until recently, with the 1880 population of 228 only increasing to 1,065 by 1950. (Durwood Barbour.)

Harward Building, Apex, N. C.

Various businesses operated in Apex in the early 1900s, including a grocery store, a drug store, a bank, a newspaper, and a tobacco market. W.H. Harward, after whom the Harward Building was named, operated a mercantile business and two different drug stores over the years. The Harward Building, at the corner of East Chatham and South Salem Streets, presently houses a florist shop and an automotive parts store.

Scenes of many small towns were captured by itinerant photographers, who offered to make these cards for local merchants to sell in their stores. This card of Apex's Graded School was made especially for the A.V. Baucom Pharmacy. Real photo postcards of small towns, like this one, are much-sought-after collectibles. (Durwood Barbour.)

This real photo card features the town hall. The card was probably made at the same time as the card of the Apex Graded School . Wonder how many other Apex real photo cards were in the set? (Durwood Barbour.)

Rural communities often provided a place for teachers to stay and take their meals during the school year. Most of the teachers in these early days were single females. This 1910 house at 209 Hughes Street, not far from the school, served as a teacherage during the 1930s and '40s. The structure has since been renovated and returned to use as a private residence.

Apex got a new high school in 1922 to replace an older building destroyed by fire. Courses for high school seniors in those days included third year Latin, English Composition and Rhetoric, United States History, Plain and Solid Geometry, and Botany. When Apex High School moved to its present campus on Laura Duncan Road, this building became part of a middle school campus. It was demolished in 1984 to make room for a new middle school building.

Cary, incorporated in 1871, was named after former Ohio congressman and temperance advocate, Samuel Fenton Cary. As early as 1870 Cary had a private high school, or academy, for male and female students. Students came from all parts of North Carolina and other southern states and were housed in dormitories on the school grounds. North Carolina's first state-supported public high school was established in Cary in 1907. The school shown on this card, postmarked January 7, 1915, was the second building to occupy the school grounds at the south end of Academy Street. This building was replaced in 1939 by a third building, which is part of the present campus of the Cary Elementary School. (Durwood Barbour.)

Workmen pose in front of the nearly completed building in Cary, which served both as a dormitory for students and as a home for teachers over the years. The structure was located near the high school on Academy Street. (Ed Williams.)

On April 6, 1871, just three days after Cary was incorporated, the town's first Methodist church was chartered, The first church had thirty-five members, while the present church, now called First United Methodist Church, has over twenty-nine hundred members. Located at Academy and Waldo Streets near downtown Cary, the original wooden church was encased in brick in 1923 and since then several additions have been added. (Peggy Holliday.)

Knotty Pine Motor Court
U. S. Highway No. 1 and 64
2 Miles South of Cary — 10 Miles South of Raleigh
Cary, North Carolina

Efforts to locate old cards of the Cary business district included dozens of phone calls and an article in the *Cary Times* asking for help. Since we were unsuccessful in finding older cards of Cary, here is the linen card from the 1940s advising motorists that the Knotty Pine Motor Court had eighteen new and modern units. The rooms were air-conditioned, had private baths, and were furnished with Beautyrest mattresses. (Manuscript Collection, Duke University.)

Stephen Fuquay discovered the "springs" while plowing one hot day in the 1850s. The water from the springs was cool, refreshing, and later was found to contain beneficial minerals. The village that grew up around the springs was incorporated as Fuquay Springs in 1909. In 1963, Fuquay Springs combined with the nearby community of Varina to form the present town of Fuquay-Varina. This card was postmarked August 24, 1909. (Durwood Barbour.)

The Raleigh and Southport Railroad, which ran trains in and out of Fuquay each day, brought throngs to visit the town's springs. Visitors drank the water, stuffed themselves with food, and returned home feeling refreshed. The water also was bottled and "advertised as helpful for rheumatism, indigestion and other ailments." The building in the foreground is a dance pavilion; just behind was the drink stand. (Manuscript Collection, Duke University.)

Some visitors to Fuquay stayed overnight at one of the town's two hotels. This view of the hotel operated by A.G. Blanchard was postmarked on August 5, 1908, and sent to a lady living on South Saunders Street in Raleigh. (Durwood Barbour.)

OLD SOUTHERN MANSION
FUQUAY SPRINGS, N. C.

This "Old Southern Mansion" is the kind of house many would expect to find on postcards of North Carolina. Although there were a few country mansions built, most people lived in much more modest quarters. The home shown was designed by architect Charles Pearson and built for James Beale Johnson about 1906. Recently renovated, it is located on Johnson Pond Road, just down the road from the new Fuquay Elementary School.

The town of Garner, to the southeast of Raleigh, was originally incorporated in 1883 as Garner Station; twenty-two years later it was incorporated under its present name. In this real photo card of Main Street, the railroad tracks are on the left and the town's stores on the right. These were the days before hard-surfaced roads. (Kaye Whaley.)

One of the early businesses in Garner was Montague's Drugstore on Main Street. To the right is the residence of George Montague, the druggist, and on the left is the home of Dr. J.S. Buffaloe, a longtime Garner physician. The message on the back of the card, postmarked August 31, 1910, reads: " Dr. Mann, will stop here on Tuesday, Aug. 6th, about 5, or 6 o'clock P. M. If you can be here at that time he would be glad to adjust your glasses. Most respectfully, MONTAGUE." (Kaye Whaley.)

Garner High School, shown here, was a frame structure located on the corner of Pearl and Main Streets. A building at this location served as the town's high school until 1923, at which time it was converted to an elementary school. The Lion's Ballpark now occupies much of this site. A comparison of the handwriting and numbering system on the face of these Garner cards with the real photo cards of Apex suggests they were the products of the same publisher. (Kaye Whaley.)

For more than sixty years, the congregation of Garner's Methodist Church worshiped in this building, which was constructed in 1892 on the corner of Main and Griffin Streets. When the Methodist Church moved in 1959 to its new home on Oak Circle, just off Vandora Springs Road, their old church was sold to the Wake Baptist Church. The building, shown here on a real photo card, was taken down in the 1970s. (Kaye Whaley.)

Holly Springs, incorporated in 1877, took its name from a natural spring located near a large holly tree in the southwestern part of the county. The public high school, one of the first in Wake County, was built in 1907. This view is believed to be an architectural rendering of the school. (Jane and George Lasley.)

Holly Springs High School, Holly Springs, N. C.

This divided back card shows the Holly Springs High School after an addition was completed about 1915. The building was converted into an elementary school in 1947 and razed in 1974.

Visitors to North Carolina may be surprised to learn that Wake Forest University is not located in the small Wake County town of Wake Forest, but 100 miles to the west in Winston-Salem. This, however, has not always been the case. Wake Forest College operated from 1834 to 1956 in the town of the same name just a few miles north of Raleigh. When the college moved, the campus was purchased as a home for the Southeastern Baptist Theological Seminary. Campus scenes of Wake Forest College are shown on the petals of this very collectible pansy card. (North Carolina Museum of History.)

The Old College Building, which for nearly a century was the center of campus activity, is on the left on this early 1900s view of the Wake Forest campus. The building was destroyed by fire in 1934. Stealey Hall, containing campus administrative offices, now occupies the site.

The Heck-Williams Building, on the right, was dedicated in September of 1879. The upper story of the central section was used for the college library, the lower section for a reading room. The north wing housed science, and mathematics was in the south wing. Heck-Williams was razed in 1957 to make way for the Denny Library Building. (Durwood Barbour.)

The Row   Wake Forest College, N. C.

Note how the people in this view of the campus all are wearing suits and hats or caps. If they were students, things certainly have changed. This card was postmarked August 4, 1929, and sent to Mr. Nick Jones in Curdsville, Virginia. The message, in part, reads, "How's life and all it's essentials with you. Evelyn and I are here in school having a grand time. Leaving for home next week. Be good! Myra." (Peggy Holliday.)

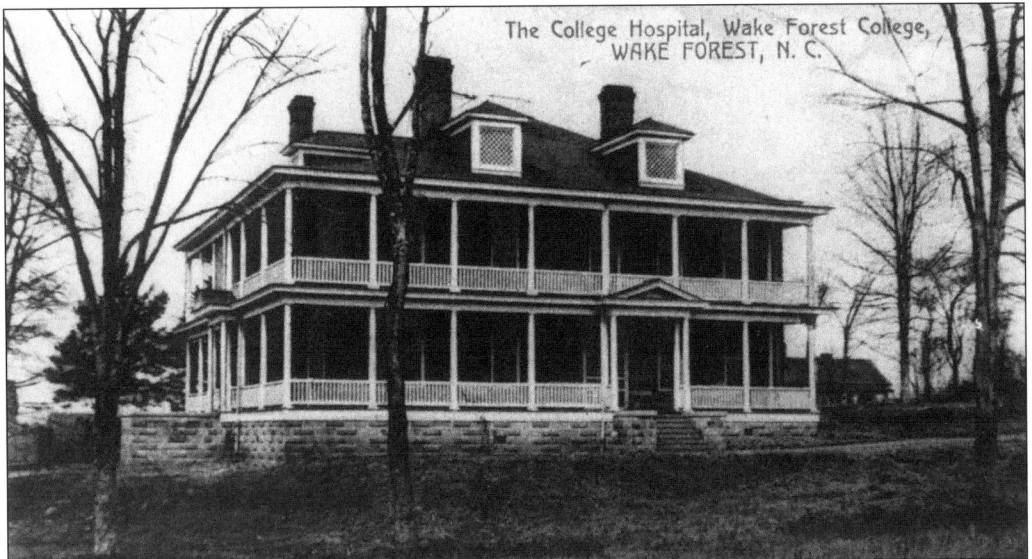

The College Hospital, Wake Forest College, WAKE FOREST, N. C.

The College Hospital was completed in September of 1906 as an infirmary for Wake Forest's two-year medical program. The first floor had a general ward, kitchen, dining room, and four other rooms. Located on the second floor were eight rooms, including an operating room and a separate ward for contagious diseases. The total cost of the concrete block building was $7,500. The site is now occupied by Lolley Hall on the southwest corner of the campus. (Durwood Barbour.)

This view of the 1906 Wake Forest College baseball team is a winner in spite of the writing on the face and the small tear in the upper right corner. This same view was published in the 1907 edition of the college's yearbook, *The Howler*. The members of the team are, from left to right: (front row) Goodwyn (center field), Couch (second base), Richardson (left field); (middle row) Hamrick (center field), Turner, E. (pitcher), Smith (captain and third base), Turner, J. (first base); (back row) Dunn (manager), Beverly (right field), White (pitcher), Holding (substitute), and Benton (short stop). The coach, not shown, was J. Richard Crozier. (Ed Williams.)

Ten years later it was the Glee Club and Orchestra's turn to be featured on a postcard. This unused real photo card has an AZO stamp box, but the publisher is not specified. This same view was published in the 1917 edition of *The Howler*, but the members of this musical group were not identified.

119

No visit to Wake Forest is complete without a drive down Faculty Avenue (now called North Main Street) to see the three dozen or so old homes in the historic district. Visible on the left are the white columns of the Brewer-Hastings House, which began as a log cabin built in 1840. Later it was enlarged to form this "English Basement" house.

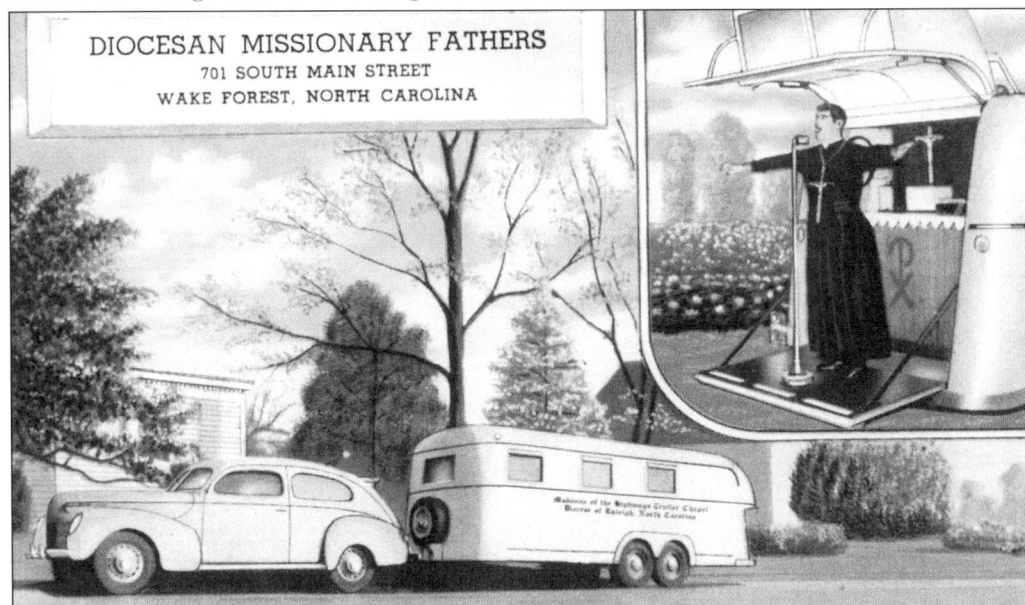

The caption on the back of this linen card explains what the Diocesan Missionary Fathers were doing in the primarily Baptist town of Wake Forest: "The Madonna of the Highways Trailer Chapel is a motor chapel owned by the Catholic Diocese of Raleigh, North Carolina, and operated throughout the state by the Diocesan Missionary Fathers. Designed by Geo. F. Chaplin it was built in 1948 and paid for by generous friends of the missions. It has an altar which can be used interiorly or exteriorly, a confessional, stations of the cross, and all church equipment besides living quarters and accommodations for two priests. A public address system, radio and Victrola equipment as well as motion picture projector help the missionaries bring to Catholic and non-Catholics in rural areas and in small towns, the Word of God. It was dedicated by Bishop Waters at Wilmington, N.C. in May 1948. You are invited to visit the Chapel on the road, or at our home in Wake Forest, N.C."

Incorporated in 1903, Wendell was named in honor of the poet and physician, Oliver Wendell Holmes. When the railroad came through, the conductors and porters sang out "Wen-dell," stressing both syllables. Locals still do, which makes it easy to spot a newcomer to the town. The broad main street was laid out by driving four two-horse teams abreast the length of Main Street. By the time this picture was taken in the late 1930s, Wendell had a well-developed business district.

The printed message on the back reads, "P. S.—I have enjoyed a visit to the North Carolina's exhibit at the New York World's Fair. You must be sure to see it." This suggests the card was given away at the Fair and explains the chamber of commerce message on the front.

As in the case of many North Carolina small towns, there were schools in the Wendell area long before there was a town. Nevertheless, the structure shown here must have been a source of community pride when it was completed in 1911. The four students in the class of 1915 were the first to graduate from the Wendell High School. After it closed in 1965, the building served for several years as an elementary school. It since has been taken down to make room for a new building. (Durwood Barbour.)

The fourth grade class at Wendell taught by Miss Mildred Beamer in 1932 lined up in front of the school. Count the students and you will see that the teacher must have had her hands full. One of the students in the photograph recalls that the other fourth grade class, 4B, was just as large.

Wakefield and Zebulon in eastern Wake County joined forces in 1907 to build a new school on 10 acres of land midway between the two towns. The name for the school was formed using the first syllable of Wakefield and the last from Zebulon. Wakelon High School, along with Cary High School in the western part of the county, became a farm-life school in 1914. The idea was to operate a model farm and household and to teach students agriculture, mechanics, and domestic science. When the high school closed in 1970, the school became Zebulon Elementary School. Later the building was sold to Glaxo and recently was completely renovated. This card is postmarked April 2, 1915. (Durwood Barbour.)

Accommodations were provided for students attending Wakelon High School who lived too far away to commute each day. These were the days before hard-surface highways and motorized school buses. This building was later converted to a teacherage. The Albertype card was published by the Citizens Drug Company of Zebulon. (Durwood Barbour.)

The area around Zebulon boomed when the railroad between Raleigh and Wilson was completed in 1907, the same year the town was incorporated. Named after North Carolina's Civil War governor, Zebulon Baird Vance, the town grew rapidly as shown by this view taken in about 1930. This is another Albertype card published by the Citizens Drug Company. (Durwood Barbour.)

The Hotel Whitley was originally built as a home for the Michael Whitley family. The eighteen-room white frame structure was transformed into a boarding house when many new residents needed a place to stay while their homes were being built. The hotel, located on the northeast corner of Arendell Avenue and Horton Street, was torn down in 1920. (Durwood Barbour.)

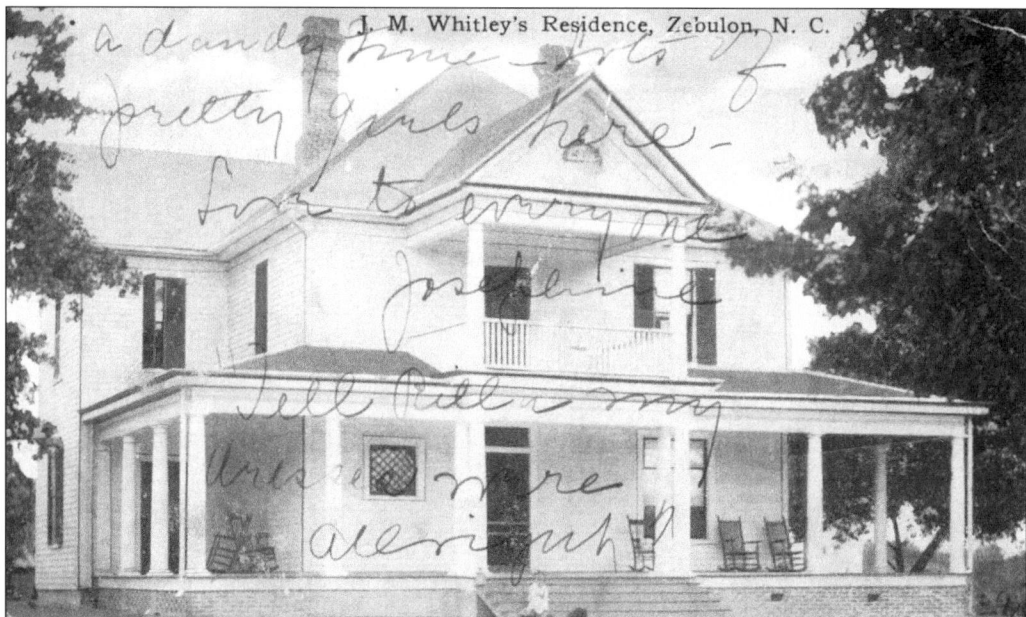

Only a dozen years after Zebulon was incorporated, the city had several beautiful homes, including the J.M. Whitley Residence. This card was mailed in March of 1915 to a gentleman in Louisburg, perhaps a college student there, and signed Josephine. The message, which starts on the back and continues on to the front, reads, "Can't you bring a crowd over to the Ball Game this afternoon? I'm having a dandy time—lots of pretty girls here. Love to everyone." How could a message reach Louisburg in time for the gentleman to go to Zebulon to a ball game the same day? Answer—the card was put aboard a train going to Louisburg, as evidenced by its RPO (Railroad Post Office) cancellation.

North Carolina for many years has been one of the leading textile states in the nation. It is not surprising then to learn that one of Zebulon's first industries was a hosiery mill. Organized in 1906 with T.J. Horton as president, the mill was constructed and in full production by 1907. It was not long before the mill was employing a hundred workers and producing six hundred pairs of hose daily. This card was postmarked December 2, 1911, and mailed to a gentleman in nearby Louisburg. (Manuscript Collection, Duke University.)

Two major crops grown in eastern North Carolina at the turn of the century were tobacco and cotton. The Zebulon Cotton Oil Company was established in 1908 near the railroad tracks just west of the business district. Within five years, the company employed twenty-five workers and processed about 30 tons of seed each day. The message on the back of this card, postmarked March 25, 1910, reads, "Went over to the mill last week. They make the meal and crude oil." (Durwood Barbour.)

125

The first Zebulon Baptist Church building was originally in Wakefield. Shortly after Zebulon incorporated in 1907, the building was partially dismantled and moved on log rollers to land donated by Martha Horton on the corner of Sycamore and Church Streets in Zebulon. The structure shown here burned to the ground when lightning struck the steeple in 1920. A new Baptist church, on the corner of Arendell and Gannon Avenues, was completed in 1924. (Bill Murphy.)

Life in the small towns and rural areas of the county had its pleasures, and during the summer months old mill ponds were a favorite with swimmers. For as long as even the oldest residents can remember, there has been a Lake Myra on Wendell Road (now called Poole Road) just a couple of miles west of Wendell. And you still can stop by the store for a cold drink and some good conversation, or rent a boat to try the fishing. (Durwood Barbour.)

Index

Cats and flowers have long been favorite subjects with postcard publishers and this greeting card combines both. Although general greeting cards are among the least expensive cards to collect, those from a particular city are much more in demand. (Sarah Pope.)